Ellen Johnson Sirleaf

OHIO SHORT HISTORIES OF AFRICA

This series of Ohio Short Histories of Africa is meant for those who are looking for a brief but lively introduction to a wide range of topics in African history, politics, and biography, written by some of the leading experts in their fields.

Ellen Johnson Sirleaf

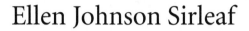

Pamela Scully

OHIO UNIVERSITY PRESS

ATHENS

Ohio University Press, Athens, Ohio 45701
ohioswallow.com
© 2016 by Ohio University Press
All rights reserved

Printed in the United States of America
Ohio University Press books are printed on acid-free paper ⊗ ™

Cover design by Joey Hi-Fi

26 25 24 23 22 21 20 19 18 17 16   5 4 3 2 1

Library of Congress Cataloging-in-Publication Data
Names: Scully, Pamela, author.
Title: Ellen Johnson Sirleaf / Pamela Scully.
Other titles: Ohio short histories of Africa.
Description: Athens : Ohio University Press, 2016. | Series: Ohio
  short histories of Africa | Includes bibliographical references and
  index.
Identifiers: LCCN 2015042165| ISBN 9780821422212 (pb : alk.
paper) | ISBN
  9780821445600 (pdf)
Subjects: LCSH: Johnson-Sirleaf, Ellen, 1938– | Women
  presidents—Liberia—Biography. | Presidents—Liberia—Biography. |
  Liberia—Politics and government—1980– | Liberia—Biography.
Classification: LCC DT636.53.J64 .S38 2016 | DDC 966.62031092—dc23
LC record available at http://lccn.loc.gov/2015042165

Contents

Illustrations

Figures

Maps

Acknowledgments

Thank you to Gill Berchowitz of Ohio University Press for her support of this project. I also very much appreciate the guidance of the two anonymous reviewers. Olivia Hendricks did sterling work on the copyediting, as did Ingrid Meintjes, who helped prepare the manuscript. The Institute for Developing Nations at Emory University and the Carter Center facilitated my engagement with Liberia over the years. I am very grateful. I appreciate all I have learned from friends and colleagues in Liberia and who work on Liberia. Special thanks to Deborah Harding for her kindness. This book is in honor of all who are working to build a strong and peaceful Liberia.

Abbreviations

ACDL	Association for Constitutional Democracy
ECOMOG	ECOWAS Monitoring Group
ECOWAS	Economic Community of West African States
INGO	international nongovernmental organization
INPFL	Independent National Patriotic Front of Liberia
LAP	Liberian Action Party
LNP	Liberia National Police
LURD	Liberians United for Reconciliation and Democracy
MODEL	Movement for Democracy in Liberia
MOJA	Movement for Justice in Africa
NDPL	National Democratic Party of Liberia
NGO	nongovernmental organization
NPFL	National Patriotic Front of Liberia
PAL	Progressive Alliance of Liberia

TRC	Truth and Reconciliation Commission of Liberia
ULIMO	United Liberation Movement of Liberia for Democracy
UN	United Nations
UNDP	United Nations Development Programme
UNICEF	United Nations Children's Fund
UNIFEM	United Nations Development Fund for Women
UNMIL	United Nations Mission in Liberia
WIPNET	Women in Peacebuilding Network
WLMAP	Women of Liberia Mass Action for Peace
WONGOSOL	Women's NGO Secretariat of Liberia

Introduction

On Friday, October 7, 2011, the Nobel Peace Prize committee took a step into history by awarding the prize to three women from Africa, two of them relatively unknown activists at the time. The committee presented the award to Ellen Johnson Sirleaf (president of Liberia), Leymah Gbowee (Liberia), and Tawakkol Karman (Yemen) "for their non-violent struggle for the safety of women and for women's rights to full participation in peace-building work."[1] The previous time that the Nobel committee had made the award to three individuals was nearly twenty years earlier, in 1994, when the Nobel Peace Prize was awarded to three high-profile leaders in Middle East politics: Yasser Arafat, Shimon Peres, and Yitzhak Rabin. With the 2011 award, the prize committee affirmed the growing international commitment to women's participation in peace building, exemplified by the UN Security Council Resolution 1325 of 2000, on women, war, and peace.[2]

In its official statement, the Nobel committee said, "We cannot achieve democracy and lasting peace in the world unless women obtain the same opportunities

Liberia. Map No. 3775 Rev. 9, September 2014, United Nations.

as men to influence developments at all levels of society." The most famous of these new laureates was Ellen Johnson Sirleaf, then campaigning for her second term as president of Liberia. The Nobel committee said of her: "Sirleaf is Africa's first democratically elected female president. Since her inauguration in 2006, she has contributed to securing peace in Liberia, to promoting economic and social development, and to strengthening the position of women."

For most of Liberia's history few people outside West Africa even knew about the country. If they had heard of Liberia, they usually knew two things: that African Americans associated with missions colonized the country in the mid-nineteenth century, and that in the 1990s and early 2000s militias in Liberia's civil war perpetrated terrible human rights abuses involving child soldiers and sexualized violence. However, such associations have receded. In 2008, the rather romantic film *Pray the Devil Back to Hell*, which chronicled women's role in ending the Liberian war, won the award for Best Documentary at the Tribeca Film Festival. The film received many subsequent awards and was also shown on PBS, introducing a wider audience to the issues of war, peace, and women's rights in Liberia.

Today Liberia is famous for having two Nobel Peace Prize winners, Sirleaf and Leymah Gbowee, head of the women's peace movement, for having the first elected woman president on the African continent, and for being a hub of experiments making women's rights part of the agenda for transitional justice and post-conflict reconstruction. When this book was being written, Liberia had also become the epicenter of the world's largest and most critical Ebola epidemic in history. Ebola revealed the limits of governance in Liberia and citizens' distrust of Sirleaf in her second term, but it also showed the incredible discipline of Liberians who made their country the first in the region to be declared free of Ebola by changing greeting and burial practices, among others. History will remember Ellen Johnson Sirleaf as a landmark and potentially game-changing president of Liberia and a force for women's rights in the international community. Whether her legacy will be remembered for changing the fundamental tensions and issues that have plagued Liberia is less certain.

For all these reasons there is immense interest in both Liberia and Ellen Johnson Sirleaf. The UN and virtually every nongovernmental organization in the world have been working in Liberia since 2003, especially on issues of sexual violence and rule of law. These organizations include the International Red Cross, the International Rescue Committee, UNIFEM (now UN Women), the Carter Center, Doctors without Borders, and many others. Their presence has helped bring Liberia into international news and has also created a conversation on Liberia that inspires young people to know more about the country.

Sirleaf's life speaks to many of the key themes facing the twenty-first century: the rise of women as a force to be reckoned with in national and international politics, the challenges of reconciling indigenous rights and experiences with national laws and urban dominance (a particular theme of Liberian history and contemporary life), the rise of ravaging civil wars and sexual violence, and the challenges of transitional justice in building a postconflict society. In 2014 Liberia also became known as the place that the deadly Ebola virus metastasized: Liberia began to implode under the weight of the disease and poor infrastructure. Ebola cast a shadow over Sirleaf's legacy. The government's authoritarian and inept handling of the disease revealed the enduring challenges facing this postconflict country and the limits of Sirleaf's technocratic approach to government in a country where so many had no access to the basic political and economic infrastructure, and where the ongoing divide between elites and other citizens continued to be a marked feature of Liberian life. However, Liberia's victory over this Ebola outbreak also can be seen as part of Sirleaf's achievement. As ever, writing history as it happens leaves much room for ambiguity.

Sirleaf's life and career exemplify the move of women into the highest echelons of international human rights. Her biography also is the story of a woman from a small country in West Africa, whose terrible civil war in the 1990s and early 2000s brought it to international attention, and who navigated her way through complex political terrain for much of her career. Her biography is thus closely linked to the story of Liberia and to the story of women's rights as international rights. Those are themes I develop in the chapters that follow.

1

Growing Up in Two Worlds

Ellen Johnson Sirleaf was born Ellen Johnson, in Monrovia, the capital of Liberia, on October 29, 1938. Today, Liberia has just over 4 million people and covers 43,000 square miles. On the West Coast of Africa, it shares borders with Sierra Leone, Guinea, and Côte d'Ivoire. It has 350 miles of wonderful coastline and a varied environment that includes tropical rain forests, plains, and mountains. It has two major seasons: the dry season (November to April) and the wet season (May to October). The wet season is hot and wet—monsoon-like, making travel difficult. The majority of the population is indigenous (there are some twenty indigenous languages) and lives in rural areas and villages following patrilineal lines of descent. In the North, secret societies for both men and women, the Poro and the Sande, help structure political and social relationships and provide avenues to power. In the South, secret societies do not hold sway, but women have long enjoyed political and social authority.

The Republic of Liberia is one of the oldest independent states in Africa, dating back to 1847. English is the official language, and a patois, Liberian English, is the lingua franca. This is because Liberia was founded through interactions with America. Five percent of Liberia's population traces its heritage to people of American descent. This Americo-Liberian group includes descendants of freed people from the Caribbean and the Americas who settled in the nineteenth century as well as Africans seized by the British navy from slave ships after the abolition of the British Atlantic slave trade and known as "Congo."

Liberia's founding was thus similar to that of neighboring Sierra Leone: free people of African descent looked to Africa to realize freedom. In the United States of America, freed people found strange bedfellows with whites who sought to move people of African descent far away from America. Different groups thus had various motivations for settling what would become Liberia: from longing to return to the continent, philanthropic interests, and racism about the increasing presence of emancipated and manumitted people of African descent in the United States. Although missionary societies sponsored the founding of Liberia, the US government backed their efforts; most notably, President James Monroe supported a missionary initiative to settle newly freed slaves. White Southern missionary societies were keen to repatriate people of African descent to Africa so that they did not stay in the United States. The American Colonization Society was the most prominent of these societies.

In the early 1820s, the ACS bought a "36 mile long and 3 mile wide" strip of coastal land for trade goods, supplies, weapons, and rum worth approximately $300, probably at gunpoint, from the Bassa and Dey societies of the West African coast.[1] The colonization of the land that was to become Liberia began. Between 1822 and 1892, the society sent 16,000 Americans to places along the coast. From the 1820s through the 1840s, various other branches settled different areas of the coast, including Cape Palmas and Maryland in the South. By 1848, four Christian denominations were established in Monrovia: Methodists, Episcopalians, Presbyterians, and Methodist Episcopalians.[2] The Commonwealth of Liberia, established in 1838 and still under the control of the ACS, derived most of its income from taxes levied on African and British traders. These taxes became a source of tension with the British government. As a result, in 1847, Americo-Liberians voted to be independent. At this time, Liberia consisted of a 45-mile-wide strip of territory with most Americo-Liberians, and Congo, living in Monrovia.

War with indigenous societies continued through much of the nineteenth century, although slowly settlers established control over the societies of the interior. As early as 1869, the Department of the Interior was created to administer affairs of what was known as the "hinterland." This rule can be thought of as a form of internal colonialism, in which settlers levied taxes on communities in the interior and ruled through force, relying on the Liberian Frontier Force. In 1907, this system of government was further developed, in a manner akin to the British policy of "indirect rule." Chiefs were made responsible for collecting taxes and putting down uprisings. The Liberian government replaced hereditary chiefs and replaced them with government functionaries and created sixteen groups that separated existing political units and affiliations. The intention was "to prevent the formation of alliances that might challenge the government." Indirect rule also excluded Africans from Liberian citizenship, since they had to renounce their "tribal" affiliation in order to participate in Liberian national political life. The system thereby widened the division between Americo-Liberians and the indigenous peoples.[3] The conditions for tension between different Liberian groups, and most markedly between Americo-Liberians and indigenous Liberians, thus were woven into the very fabric of rule. This tension was a primary source for the civil wars that plagued Liberia from 1980 through 2003, It was one of the greatest challenges inherited by Sirleaf when she became president in 2006.

Up to the 1920s, Liberia's economy was primarily agricultural. A shipbuilding business in Monrovia flourished up to the late nineteenth century, when competition from steamships ended it. In the early decades of the twentieth century, Liberia thus struggled to find its economic footing, but in the 1920s, the solution presented itself, with long-term consequences for the country. In 1926, Firestone, the big rubber company, signed a lease with the government to rent up to a million acres of land at six cents an acre for ninety-nine years, paying a 1 percent tax on the gross value of exported rubber. This put the company in control of about 4 percent of the entire country's landmass. Firestone also got the rights to any natural resources discovered on its concession and was exempted from taxes, with some exceptions. The government, in its turn, ensured a labor force to work on the plantations.

Since rubber trees take seven years to grow, the agreement did not immediately help the government, but in time, the Firestone agreement became the single most important factor in maintaining the Liberian economy. The terms of the agreement in effect made the Liberian government handmaiden to Firestone: The company, under its subsidiary the Finance Corporation of Liberia, with the support of the US government, forced a loan of $5 million to the Liberian government. This put the Liberian government in debt to the company and vastly hampered the country's economic independence. In addition, the government was not permitted to sign any new concessionary agreements without the consent of the company. The end result was that Firestone was given carte blanche and the Liberian government became the purveyor of labor to Firestone. The government in effect began to manage forced labor.

Reports of forced labor began circulating in the 1920s and concluded in a commission organized by the

League of Nations in 1930. The report stated that slavery did not exist, but the report did raise the practice of "pawning" as an issue of concern. Pawning occurred primarily in the rural areas, where families pawned a child or relative as payment for a debt. In addition, wealthy families in Monrovia practiced their own system in which they took children from rural families into their homes as servants or wards. This latter practice both depended on the inequalities between the settlers and other Liberians and also paradoxically helped expand the Americo-Liberian elite. As one author put it, "The acceptance of tribal children as wards has long been considered a Christian duty by Americo-Liberians." In the 1960s, "a great many of the educated Monrovians today . . . were taken into Americo-Liberian families during this period."[4]

Sirleaf was born into precisely that milieu: both her parents had been fostered into Americo-Liberian families. Her paternal grandfather was a chief in Bomi County, just to the north of Monrovia. As was the common practice among rural families, he sent his son Karnley, Sirleaf's father, to Monrovia to live with a Congo family so he could learn English and participate in life there. Sirleaf's father went on to become the first indigenous person to sit in the House of Representatives. Sirleaf's maternal grandfather was a German, who returned to Germany during the First World War. He left his daughter Martha with her mother, Juah Sarwee, a farmer in Sinoe County in the south of the country. Like Sirleaf's father, Sirleaf's mother, Martha, was also sent to Monrovia. Martha became the ward of a family called the Dunbars, who were one of the oldest settler families in Liberia. She changed her name to Martha Dunbar.

These family connections meant that although Sirleaf grew up in the 1940s and early 1950s in the only really big town in Liberia, she spent the summers of her childhood in the rural areas and thus had intense contact with her indigenous roots. In the summers she would go to the home of her paternal grandmother north of Monrovia. There she learned to speak some of the local language, Gola, and to experience life with no running water. She spent time collecting both water and food and socializing with other people in the village.

When Sirleaf was growing up, Monrovia was a small town, dominated by churches and the social life of the Americo-Liberian elite. It was small enough that people walked to school and the shops, and as Sirleaf herself remembers, also traveled by canoe to places further afield. The first census of Monrovia was taken in 1956, a year after Sirleaf graduated from high school. The population was 42,000 then, though three years later it was 53,000. In a survey conducted by Merran Fraenkel in 1959, some six out of every ten adults in Monrovia had moved there since 1948. This shows great mobility between the rural areas and the capital in this postwar era. People perceived as Americo-Liberian—that is, born or adopted into the Americo-Liberian elite—accounted for some 16 percent of the population. Businessmen and

Aerial view of downtown Monrovia, Liberia. 1954. Photo by John T. Smith Jr. in *A History of Flying and Photography: In the Photogrammetry Division of the National Ocean Survey, 1919–1979.*

traders, mostly from the growing Lebanese community, also were by then a key component of Monrovia's population, and nearly as many Ghanaians also lived in the city (1,193). Government remained a key employer in Monrovia. There was also a growing business sector in construction and commerce, owned primarily by foreigners, which employed nearly as many people as the government.[5]

Sirleaf grew up on Benson Street, one of the major streets in the city. The American Embassy sits at the end of Benson Street on the corner of United Nations Drive. Sirleaf was the third of four children and recalls a very happy childhood, which saw the family becoming increasingly wealthy as her father moved up in the Tubman government. Her mother opened an elementary school, which Sirleaf and her sister Jennie attended, and also became a Presbyterian preacher. By the 1940s and '50s, churches proliferated in Monrovia. By far the largest number of Monrovians attended the Methodist Episcopal Church. The next-largest denomination was Roman Catholic, followed by smaller numbers of the other denominations, including the Liberian Baptist Missionary and Educational Convention, the National Baptist Mission USA, AME and AME Zion churches, and the Presbyterians. In this era a relatively small number of people in Monrovia were Muslim, though the numbers grew with the movement of rural people into the city. The 1959 survey undertaken by Fraenkel showed some 13 percent of adults interviewed identified themselves as Muslim and 59 percent as Christian.[6]

Christianity was a marker of civilized status and upward mobility in the Monrovia in which Sirleaf grew up. Discrimination against Muslims, who were not allowed to hold government posts, contributed to the movement of young people to Christianity. During this era, most Muslims in Monrovia were uneducated. Conversion to Christianity and education happened at the same time in schools. Although Christianity was an essential ingredient for being part of the Americo-Liberian or "civilized" community, it was membership in particular churches that was crucial. Most of the key Christian denominations had a church in the center of town and a smaller building in the suburbs. The Protestant Episcopal Church was the "favoured church of the elite,"[7] although Sirleaf's parents were Presbyterians.

During her early life Sirleaf had the opportunity to learn about the different religious traditions of the country. In Monrovia she attended church, but back in Bomi County many people in her father's village were Muslim. People also practiced indigenous religions. Sirleaf's mother was a preacher in the Presbyterian Church, and her children went with her as she preached around Liberia. Sirleaf's childhood experiences of diversity in income, religion, and geography in some ways prepared her more than some other Liberians whose experiences were limited to Monrovia. As she writes in her autobiography, "My feet are in two worlds—the world of poor rural women with no respite from hardship and the world of accomplished Liberian professionals, for whom the United States is a second and beloved home. I draw strength from both."[8]

Sirleaf did well at school and attended the prestigious College of West Africa in Monrovia from 1948 to 1955, graduating with a diploma in economics and accounting. This Methodist high school, founded in 1904, was a product of mission education in the nineteenth century. The school's prestige remains. In 2011, the Liberia Annual Conference approved the CWA as a United Methodist Historic Site, one of only six sites outside the United States.[9] At school, Sirleaf excelled in academics as well as sports. But during her high school years, her father had a stroke, which changed the family's fortunes and led to Sirleaf feeling that her educational opportunities after school were now limited. However, Sirleaf was fortunate to come of age at the time when women were gaining political rights in Liberia.

One of President Tubman's achievements was to open up opportunities for women. In 1947, one hundred years after the official founding of the country of Liberia, women received the vote. Women soon started organizing to champion further rights. Under the leadership of the newly formed National Liberian Social and Political Movement, the act was amended to allow women to hold any political office. Americo-Liberian women in particular were able to take advantage of these new opportunities and soon held many posts in both government and civil society. For example, in an article published in 1968, Angie E. Brooks, then president of the Trusteeship Council of the United Nations, listed a number of women in high government positions at the time. These included roles such as Under Secretary for Public Works and Utilities, Assistant Secretary for Information, Secretary of the Liberian Senate, Director of American and European Affairs in the Department of State.[10] That so many women were able to get positions in government speaks mostly to the smallness of the Liberian elite, where everyone knew everyone and where relationships between key families anchored politics.

Sirleaf was thus part of a cohort of women who could aspire to participate fully as Liberian citizens as well as enter government. However, when Sirleaf was growing up, young women were expected to start a family, and that is what she did. She married at seventeen, in 1956. According to her autobiography, while her wealthier friends went off to college in the United States, Sirleaf wondered how she was going to fare. In this context, marriage seemed a way to a secure future, and it presented itself in the form of James ("Doc") Sirleaf. He was seven years older than Ellen Johnson and had already been to the Tuskegee Institute, the famous historically black college in the United States. Ellen married James, and they had two boys, James T. and Charles Sirleaf, only some nine months apart.[11]As her autobiography recounts, for the first few years, they lived with Doc's mother, and Ellen Johnson Sirleaf worked as a secretary and later as an accountant. Then Doc got a job teaching at a school outside of Monrovia, and the family settled on a farm. Two more boys arrived before Ellen and Doc returned to Monrovia, where Doc took up the always coveted government job. Robert Sirleaf was born in 1960, and James H., known as Adamah, in 1962. For many women of the Liberian elite, the rest of their life would have been the story of working, bringing up the children, and nurturing the family. Ellen Johnson Sirleaf decided to lead a different kind of life focused on work, leadership, and nationbuilding.

Scholar and Government Employee

The 1960s and 1970s

In 1962, Ellen Johnson Sirleaf went to the United States to study. The catalyst for her going was the scholarship that Doc had received to study at the University of Wisconsin. Sirleaf saw that her school friends were faring better with higher educational opportunities. Sirleaf decided that she too needed to study in the United States. It is hard to know exactly what drives individuals, but clearly Sirleaf believed in herself from a young age and was driven to achieve. She overcame the kinds of obstacles (domestic violence, imprisonment, exile) that would have derailed a more timid personality. With perhaps only a hint of irony, Sirleaf's autobiography is titled *This Child Will Be Great*, evidence of a strong ego. Indeed, the book is framed to show how "the path of greatness unfolded."[1]

In order to study, Sirleaf had to leave her children behind. Having to choose between taking up educational or job opportunities and staying with one's children was a common dilemma for many women across West Africa. In Sirleaf's case, going to the United States offered a number of advantages: furthering her education, thus helping the family's future, and staying with her husband. Like many Africans, Sirleaf and Doc left their children, including baby Adamah, in the care of relatives: two sons went to Doc's mother and two to Ellen's. But such separations did not come without cost: Sirleaf says while she had to do this, it did cause a "hairline fracture" in the relationship with her children, although as we will see, three of her sons have helped support her presidency in one way or another.

In moving to the United States for further study, Sirleaf joined a new wave of young Liberians who looked to the United States as a land of opportunities. The number of Liberians in the United States at that time was, however, much smaller than it would later become: only some two thousand students made their way in these years to the United States. While Doc Sirleaf studied at the University of Wisconsin, a leading state school, Sirleaf attended Madison Business College, a much smaller and less prestigious institution. Founded in the mid-nineteenth century, the college went through at least five name changes before finally closing its doors in 1998. Sirleaf received her accounting degree from the college in 1964 and continued to be a good student, attending the University of Colorado and finally receiving a master's in public administration from Harvard in 1971.

Sirleaf attended college in the 1960s, the era of civil rights, including the rise of Black Consciousness and the second wave of the feminist movement. In many ways, her career embodied the promise offered by both movements: the rights of people of African descent to lay public claim to their rights and the expansion of opportunities for women. But in both the public sphere and the private, this also was a time of tensions: Sirleaf was in the United States when President Kennedy was assassinated and when his brother Bobby was gunned down. In the private sphere of Sirleaf's life, violence also reigned. For Sirleaf these were years of increasing violence in her home, as her husband succumbed to drinking and jealousy and started attacking her. Sirleaf's personal experiences with domestic violence perhaps helped propel her later into the public sphere to address women's rights, and particularly women's rights to be free of sexual violence both in war and in peacetime, as we will see in later chapters.

Colleges and universities were the site of ferment and debate about America's role in the Vietnam War and in internationalization more generally. Students from Liberia also began to participate in politics. In the late 1960s they organized the Liberian Student Union. According to one author, Liberian students in the United States generally supported the government of William V. S. Tubman because they benefited from his financial support for education.[2] While a student, Sirleaf did not participate in these early movements; instead, she concentrated on her studies, holding her difficult marriage together, and working after school in a menial job to put food on the table. At Harvard too she focused on her studies. But once she entered the business world in later years, she began to have more interaction with the politics of the Diaspora. In 1974, Gabriel Baccus Matthews founded the Progressive Alliance of Liberia (PAL), which leaned toward socialist and Pan-Africanist policies. Sirleaf has called him the "Godfather of Liberian Democracy." Sirleaf never became a member of PAL, but she did participate in meetings when she was in the United States working for the World Bank.

Back in Liberia in the 1960s, the government was becoming enmeshed in the politics of the Cold War. Tubman was president of Liberia from 1944 to 1971, which included a long stretch of the Cold War. During that era, the United States looked to countries around the world to shore up its position vis-à-vis the Soviet Union. Liberia was just such a place. The United States had long been interested in Liberia, as evidenced by the Firestone agreement in 1926, which the US government had monitored closely. The United States signed a defense pact with Liberia as early as 1942 and built the Roberts airport to support military activity during World War II. The Voice of America's main relay station was near Monrovia, and the US Embassy compound housed the CIA's main African station.[3]

Tubman was a very popular president in Monrovia. A song popular in the 1950s, celebrating the occasion of his second inauguration, suggests that at least some residents of Monrovia were encouraged by his leadership:

"Inauguration, President Tubman, Inauguration is a time for rejoicing. He give me a house. He give me good water. President Tubman, thank you for your kindness. He give me good roads. He give me good food. President Tubman, thank you for your kindness."[4] Some of Tubman's support derived from his forging of close relations with the United States and other countries in the West, which was a mark of his presidency, along with encouraging foreign investment in Liberia through his Open Door Policy. President Tubman inaugurated the Open Door Policy in the first year of his presidency, thinking that virtually unfettered access to Liberia's natural resources and low taxes on foreign companies would stimulate investment. Foreign companies did take advantage of these options, with companies such as the Republic Steel Corporation and LAMCO building railways to their concessions in Bomi and Nimba counties. In the 1950s, Liberia had the second-highest increase in gross national product, second only to Japan's.[5] While the companies employed thousands of Liberians, well-paying jobs went to expatriates, and little was done to invest in the education or promotion of Liberian workers.[6] In her first term as president Sirleaf sought to address the unequal terms of foreign companies' relations with Liberia.

Tubman also initiated a new relationship with the interior under what he called the Unification Policy. The aim of this approach was to lessen the divide between the Americo-Liberian coast and the indigenous interior.

In 1964 the old hinterland provinces, which had been ruled through indirect rule, were given the status of counties, thus creating, at least in bureaucratic terms, an equal relationship between all people to the state. By his death in 1971, Tubman had achieved better integration of Liberia. However, property qualifications undermined the extension of the vote to indigenous citizens, and persistent inequality remained between urban elites and the majority of Liberians, who lived in the rural areas.

On returning to Liberia, Sirleaf started work in the Treasury Department in 1965. This position gave her a very good, but not very optimistic, view of the economy, which was laden with debt and dependence on foreign companies such as Firestone. During her time in the Treasury her marriage continued to crumble, and ultimately Sirleaf and her husband divorced. Two of her sons went to school; one stayed with his paternal uncle, but Rob, the third child, insisted on staying with Sirleaf. He traveled with her to the United States when she decided to continue her education. He lived with friends in South Dakota and finished high school there. This time with his mother consolidated a close relationship between the two of them. When she became president, he returned to Liberia, serving as her adviser and becoming the first head of the National Oil Company of Liberia and later chair of the First National Bank.

Sirleaf went to the University of Colorado at Boulder in 1970 for the summer to brush up her credentials, and then on to Harvard. Sirleaf's time at Harvard was transformational in her life and politics. As we have seen, Sirleaf's childhood had helped create a bridge between the two worlds of Liberia, urban and rural, the world of Americo-Liberia and the world of indigenous Liberia. She credits her time in Cambridge, Massachusetts, with educating her about the unequal history of Liberia and its connections not just with the United States but also with historical and contemporary West Africa. She returned to Monrovia in July 1971 armed with new expertise in administration and a new appreciation for the history of West Africa and its economic challenges and opportunities. She arrived just after the death of President Tubman in London from complications from surgery.

Tubman had governed Liberia for nearly thirty years. His death came at a time when revolutions were sweeping through the remaining settler colonies of Africa, including the rise of the Black Consciousness movement in South Africa, and anticolonial movements in other parts of Southern Africa. Tubman had tried to move the country forward by crafting his Open Door Policy and the Unification Policy and by relying on the new young class of educated Liberians, many of whom had traveled abroad for educational opportunities. William R. Tolbert Jr., who had served as Tubman's vice president since 1952, succeeded him in 1971 and continued to rely on the talents of the Diaspora to staff his administration.

The 1970s were the decade in which the Diaspora became a force in Liberian politics.[7] New political movements were emerging in Liberia. Sirleaf always gravitated to the mainstream, attached to government rather than revolution, an orientation that would later shape her approach as president. She was friendly, however, with activist colleagues who wanted radical reform. Faculty who had been educated overseas started the Movement for Justice in Africa (MOJA). They wanted to pursue socialist policies of redistribution to address the inequalities they saw in Liberia. Amos Sawyer, with a PhD from Northwestern University in the United States, who later was a professor of political science and dean of the College of Social Sciences at the University of Liberia, and president of the Interim Government of National Unity after the end of the civil war in the 2000s, was a founding member along with Togba Nah Roberts, an economics professor at UL. This movement was in alignment with the anticolonial movements sweeping Southern Africa at the time: The Mozambique Liberation Front (FRELIMO) and the Movement for the National Independence of Angola (MPLA), for example. As Sirleaf said, "MOJA played a pivotal role in radicalizing the urban and rural poor of Liberia, raising the issues of government corruption, advocating for the nationalization of Liberia's major businesses."[8]

However, while the Tolbert years were years of reform, the Tolbert administration was either unwilling or unable to fully address the inequalities in Liberia. Tolbert did not take the paths suggested by MOJA, although he did try to signify a new era through symbolic rejection of the formal Western attire of his predecessors in favor of open-necked suits, visits to poorer parts of Monrovia, and reform of government. But these were symbolic rather than structural reforms. Part of the difficulty of truly reforming Liberia was that it was so dependent on foreign interests. The 1926 agreement with Firestone weighed down the country. As early as 1951, for example, Firestone made in profits "three times the total income of the Liberian Treasury" even after it had paid its taxes to the Liberian government. In addition, the success of iron ore mining, which started in the 1950s, financed by investment from the United States, the Netherlands, and Sweden, also achieved great profits. Between 1951 and 1977, one mine, the Liberian Mining Company in the Bomi Hills, shipped out iron ore worth some $540 million while the Liberian government received only $84 million in return (excluding money from rents).[9]

On returning to Liberia, Sirleaf joined a wave of young professionals eager to help build the country using the skills they had acquired abroad. President Tolbert recruited Sirleaf to serve as assistant minister of finance from 1972 to 1973 and then as minister of finance in 1979. In 1972, the year that she was appointed to Tolbert's new government, Sirleaf delivered the commencement address at her high school alma mater, the College of West Africa. In that speech she criticized the government and warned that if economic disparities were not addressed Liberia would "create unbearable tensions."[10] The speech caused great consternation in the halls of the Tolbert government, in part because it criticized the administration of which Sirleaf was a part. Although she avoided public reprimand, her position in Liberia became increasingly marginal. As a result, in 1973, she sought out friends at the World Bank and took up a position as a loan officer in Washington, DC. This post offered Sirleaf a wealth of experiences that would prove crucial to the philosophy of her presidency. She met key financial players in the international economy as well as in national settings, and she developed her ideas about the impact of development dollars. After working with the World Bank, she concluded that although foreign investment and development monies came with all sorts of restrictions and created difficult relationships between governments and funders, such investments were crucial, and that the lack of capacity in many countries of the Global South meant that countries had to depend on the expertise of people from the Global North. As we will see, this conviction became central to her decisions in her first term as president of Liberia. Sirleaf's orientation toward neoliberalism with its emphasis on governance and investment rather than social justice and transformation was one of the reasons for her success in mobilizing support for Liberia. It was also, one could argue, the foundation of her alienation from the majority of Liberian citizens and the Achilles heel of her presidency.

Just two years later, Sirleaf returned to Liberia and the Tolbert government, but this time as an adviser seconded by the World Bank. She was in government, but to some extent not complicit with it. The Liberia she returned to remained divided between the Americo-Liberians who claimed to be on the side of civilization and the indigenous Liberians who sought greater participation in government and greater opportunities for advancement. Matilda Newport Day was still an official national holiday. This holiday celebrated an early settler who "saved the settlers from 'the natives'" in a battle of 1822. In 2003, a Liberian recalled,

> As a youth growing up in Monrovia, we used to assemble at Coconut Plantation each December 1 to watch the reenactment of the Battle of Fort Hill. And during the reenactment, one group of actors would dress up in native Liberian attire with their faces painted to portray native Liberian tribesmen, and the other groups of actors would dress up in Antebellum south-style outfits to portray Americo-Liberians Settlers or Pioneers. And suddenly, a woman dressed up as an old lady would appear from nowhere, light a cannon pointed directly at the actors dressed like native tribesmen (portrayed like fools in front of the cannon), and then "BOOM" the cannon goes off, and all of them would fall and pretend to die.[11]

The fact that the government marked this event with a holiday and expected all Liberians to celebrate it exemplified the tone-deafness of the Americo-Liberian elite, as well as the Tolbert administration, to the injustices and indignities that lay at the heart of the country.

Helene Cooper, writing of the 1970s, describes these divisions: "In Liberia, we cared far more about how we looked outside than about who we were inside. It was crucial to be 'Honorable'. . . . You could have a PhD from Harvard but if you were a Country man with a tribal affiliation you were still outranked in Liberian society by an Honorable with a two-bit degree from some community college in Memphis, Tennessee." Americo-Liberians associated with government lived in great style, although perhaps not many in the style of Helene Cooper's family. In her poignant memoir *The House at Sugar Beach*, she describes their family compound some eleven miles outside of Monrovia, which had air conditioning, at least seven bedrooms, and six bathrooms. The family had a family farm and a house in Spain, and the older daughter was schooled in England. Like many other Congo families, the Coopers also participated in the ward system, bringing a young woman, Eunice, to live as a companion to the young Helene. Even in 1974, "Native Liberians routinely jumped at the chance to have their children reared by Congo families" because it offered the possibility of education in a highly stratified society.[12]

The Tolbert government never really figured out how to respond creatively to the growing tide of criticism coming from PAL and MOJA. PAL was the first legal opposition party in many years in Liberia. Although Tolbert had encouraged them in this endeavor, the administration was unsettled by actual debate and criticism: this was the tradition in the history of state rule in Liberia. As part of Tolbert's plan to bring Liberia into greater communication with other African countries, he proposed that Liberia host the 1979 Organisation of African Unity summit. Doing so meant that in the years leading up to it, vast amounts of money were spent on paving roads and building a hotel and the Unity Conference Center outside Monrovia. Tensions around government spending came to a head when the price of rice, the staple food of Liberia and already subsidized by the government for that reason, went from $22 to $27 for a hundred-pound bag. The riots that broke out in response spelled the end of the Tolbert administration. PAL led the charge for cheaper rice, and a rally was organized for 3 p.m. on April 14, 1979. Forty-one deaths were documented, although there might have been a hundred more. President Tolbert arrested the leaders and instituted a commission of inquiry, which Sirleaf sat on. She was, as ever, part of government but from a critical distance.

Echoing Sirleaf's speeches about government corruption earlier in the decade, this commission also called out the administration for nepotism and called for the release of the leaders. Perhaps this forthrightness appealed to Tolbert, because shortly after the OAU summit, he appointed Sirleaf the minister of finance. Thus she was right in the middle of the government when Master Sergeant Samuel Doe launched his coup on April 12, 1980.

Liberian Opportunities and International Perils

On April 12, 1980, Master Sergeant Samuel Doe of the Liberian army launched a coup against President William R. Tolbert Jr. and his administration. As we have seen, the Tolbert administration had sought to make symbolic overtures to indigenous Liberians by eschewing the American trappings of formal attire and by trying to integrate Liberia into a Pan-African world. But this was too little and definitely too late. After more than 130 years of being relegated to second-class status and seeing wealth accumulated by a few families, some people were ready to make change happen.

Samuel Doe was the antithesis of the Congo elite: He was born on May 6, 1950, to poor parents in Tuzon, a village just north of the capital of Grand Gedeh County, which borders Côte d'Ivoire. As the County Development Report stated in 2011, "Grand Gedeh is the third largest County in Liberia and historically one of the most neglected. The over-concentration of facilities and services in Monrovia has led to the under-development of the countryside in Liberia, and Grand Gedeh County is no exception. Inadequate and non-existent basic infrastructure continues to hobble the quality of life, and this was a main contributing factor to the civil crisis." In 1984, the population of the district was 63,028 people in a landscape of slightly more than four thousand square miles, just over 9 percent of Liberia's land. Zwedru, the capital, is about 350 miles southeast of Monrovia and even to this day is accessed by only one main road, which winds its way northeast from Monrovia and then takes a turn south. So although Grand Gedeh is not in fact far from Monrovia, it is, and was, distant from access to power and influence, exemplified by the lack of a main road directly to its own capital. Grand Gedeh is rich in iron ore and gold, and it is densely forested. When Doe was growing up, people were mostly engaged in agriculture (which was profoundly disrupted by the civil war in the 1980s and beyond). Farmers grew and sold rice as well as cocoa to neighboring counties. People were also employed on palm farms and by the big logging companies that had concessions in the area.[1]

Doe was twenty-eight when he orchestrated the coup. A member of the Krahn ethnic group, the dominant ethnic group in Grand Gedeh County, he finished elementary school and then joined the Liberian army, one of the few avenues for social mobility. He was promoted to master sergeant just six months before he led the coup against Tolbert in April 1980. He also attended night school and had made it as far as his junior year by the time of the coup. In this respect, Doe took up one of the mantras of Liberian life: that education could be a vehicle for advancement. But we can assume that he also knew that as a member of an ethnic group from a far-off and neglected county, he would not get as far as he wished. He plotted the coup in secret along with others in the Armed Forced of Liberia. The former US ambassador (who had a staff of some five hundred at the US Embassy in Monrovia) says that the coup came as a surprise.[2]

In the wee hours of April 12, William R. Tolbert Jr., president of Liberia, was brutally killed while in his dressing gown. In the course of the day, other ministers, including Sirleaf, were called to appear before Doe. According to Sirleaf, Doe asked her to explain her most recent budget to one of his newly appointed staff, and thereafter he sent her home, safely, with an escort. These interviews continued for a few days. In the meantime, people attacked the Congo and looted wealthy homes, inspired by the overthrow of Tolbert's elite government. As told in her memoir, soldiers looking to attack Congo families raided Helene Cooper's house at Sugar Beach, some eleven miles from Monrovia.

While anarchy prevailed in the streets, brutality continued in the halls of power. Cabinet ministers were arrested and brought before a military tribunal of five men. The disdain many of the America-Liberian elite had shown their indigenous countrymen now turned up outside court. As soldiers dragged in the former minister of finance, the crowd apparently cried, "Who born soldier? Country woman! Who born minister? Congo woman!"[3] Doe had members of Tolbert's cabinet taken to the beach in Monrovia, where they were lined up and shot. Thirteen people were murdered. Sirleaf avoided this fate, perhaps because of her gender, perhaps because of her talent with finances, perhaps because as Doe said, Sirleaf's mother had once been kind to him (something her mother did not verify), or perhaps, as Sirleaf recounts in her biography, because she had given enough public speeches denouncing corruption in the Tolbert government to have credibility with Doe.

Doe appointed his new cabinet, including members of MOJA (Movement for Justice in Africa) and of PAL (Progressive Alliance of Liberia) whom Tolbert had put in prison for leading the opposition and inciting the rice riots. Doe's new cabinet also included Sirleaf. Clearly the choice in these early days was doing his bidding or death. Rule fell to Doe's military supporters, now called the People's Redemption Council. Sirleaf agreed to serve in the new administration as president of the Liberian Bank for Development and Investment. Operating between a rock and a hard place, or making pragmatic compromises with tyrants at least in the early days of their rule, might be described as Sirleaf's modus operandi until she became president herself. Her willingness to try for a while to work with Charles Taylor led to cries of foul during the Truth and Reconciliation Commission of Liberia (TRC) hearings.

So Sirleaf stayed to work in the Doe government even after the assassinations of cabinet ministers, the flight of her sister into exile, the suspension of the constitution, and the institution of martial law. Sirleaf justifies her decision as being in the service of her country. As she says, the Liberia that Doe seized was in tremendous debt from hosting the Organisation of African Unity and owed some $700 million in foreign debt. The coup also meant that wealthy Liberians and investors took their money out of the country. It is hard to know quite what to make of Sirleaf's decision. In one light she was an opportunist; in another, a selfless veteran of government who saw that her expertise was needed in an administration ruled by a man with talent but without much education. Clearly Sirleaf is a pragmatist. Perhaps that is the quality that helped her navigate different political terrains so successfully.

The early years of the Doe administration, although far from ideal, were peaceful enough that Leymah Gbowee, a co-winner of the Nobel Peace Prize with Sirleaf in 2011, recalls a happy childhood in Monrovia. The main thoroughfare, Tubman Road, was still lined with trees and graceful buildings, and the University of Liberia sat up on the hill across the road from the executive mansion. In the 1970s, Gbowee's father worked as chief radio technician and liaison with the United States, working at the US Embassy at the end of the street where Sirleaf grew up.[4] The United States continued its close relationship with Liberia owing to the geopolitics of the Cold

War. In Monrovia, the US Embassy collaborated with the Liberian National Security Agency.

Doe consolidated his power in part through working the politics of the Cold War. Never mind that Doe had killed almost the entire Liberian cabinet; on August 17, 1982, he went to the White House. Photographs show Doe with President Reagan and Secretary of Defense Caspar Weinberger. On that day, President Reagan spoke on the White House lawn: "Chairman Doe told me of his government's ambitious goals, including the return to democratic institutions and economic stabilization. We welcome his emphasis on bringing the benefits of development to every corner of Liberia. And today we discussed how the United States can assist Liberia in achieving these goals." Doe said he welcomed President Reagan's assurance that "we can continue to count on America's understanding and support for the fulfillment of the objectives of our revolution."[5]

The United States was indeed interested in maintaining influence over Liberia. President Jimmy Carter was the first president to visit the country (in 1978, while Tolbert was still president) since Roosevelt had stopped there briefly in 1943. Carter stayed for only four hours en route to Nigeria—but the visit signified the US desire to maintain close ties because of Liberia's strategic importance. The United States supported Doe in part because he represented a change from the oligarchy that had ruled the country since its founding. As the first indigenous president, though illegitimately in that role,

Doe spoke to the ideals of democracy embraced at least rhetorically by the Reagan administration. In addition, Doe was eager to keep those ties as close as possible. He closed the Libyan Embassy in Monrovia and opened greater diplomatic relations with Israel. As a result of this cooperation, the United States gave some $500 million to Liberia during the first five years of the Doe administration. And Doe diverted about a third of the $220 million economy into his pockets and those of his cronies.[6]

Sirleaf served a few months in the Doe government, on detachment from the World Bank. Another minister was Charles Taylor, who served as director general of the General Services Agency (which procured goods for the government) until 1983, when he was fired for embezzling a million dollars and fled to the United States. After Sirleaf gave a speech about corruption at a local school, Doe became less pleased with having her on board, and in November 1980, Sirleaf also fled to the United States, with the help of the World Bank. Sirleaf spent a short time in Washington, DC, before moving to Nairobi, Kenya, where she worked as vice president of the African regional office of Citibank.

Both these appointments put her into conversation with people in international finance and development, which would prove pivotal for the success of her first term as president in Liberia over two decades later. In Washington, while still employed by the World Bank, she connected with leading politicians, including Robert McNamara, former Secretary of Defense under Lyndon

Johnson, and head of the World Bank since 1968. In Nairobi, she was put in charge of making connections to countries that did not yet have a Citibank office. Thus she traveled in East Africa, particularly working in Uganda, where she became friends with Yoweri Museveni, now the long-lasting president of the country since 1986. While in Nairobi, Sirleaf also kept up with President Doe, visiting him when she went home to Liberia. The pull of politics was strong, and Sirleaf became involved in the Liberian election of 1985.

By the mid-1980s, the US government was becoming embarrassed by the excesses of the Doe government. As a result, they pressured Doe to hold an election, which duly happened in January 1985. Doe created an interim National Assembly and had leaders with gravitas such as Dr. Amos Sawyer draft a new constitution for Liberia. Doe did not much care for this constitution as it stipulated that a president had to be thirty-five years old. Doe was only thirty-three, so he ignored that requirement. Believing some of the hype about the beginning of a new era, Sirleaf returned to Monrovia in 1984 and started the National Democratic Party of Liberia (NDPL). But she was soon disabused of Doe's intentions to foster democracy. After giving another speech about corruption, Sirleaf found herself under house arrest and then in prison, and shortly thereafter charged with sedition. She was imprisoned with university students who had protested the arrest of their dear Professor Sawyer.

Now, Sirleaf's connection with the world financial elite paid off: people at Citibank and the World Bank began to lobby for her release. And as she says in her autobiography, even the Reagan administration came to her aid,[7] since the country to which they had already pledged millions was now looking more and more like a democratic basket case. It was also in this moment that Sirleaf began to realize the political power of Liberian women, a power that would later boost her to the presidency in 2005. Thousands of women lobbied for her release. However, they proved unable to alter the court's verdict of guilty, with the sentence of ten years in prison. But in a life full of miracles, probably all helped by a history of working in powerful positions in powerful institutions around the world, another occurred: rather than being sent to the notorious Belle Yalla prison, Sirleaf was released, along with the students.

Instead of sinking into obscurity or leaving for overseas, Sirleaf then ran for senator with the Liberian Action Party. Although it seems that the LAP won the election, President Doe delayed results until his election commission stated that the presidential party had won, by a slim 50.9 percent. Although the United States said that the election was somewhat irregular, their interest in maintaining the balance of Cold War politics meant that they continued supporting Doe. He became increasingly authoritarian, and repression became worse after an attempted coup by Thomas Quiwonkpa, one of Doe's former compatriots, in November of the same year.

Sirleaf was caught up in the aftermath of the coup, seen as a supporter of Quiwonkpa because she refused to take up her senate seat in protest of the rigged elections. Moved from one prison to another, she endured taunts and possible death, but her stature as a minister in the government and perhaps her earlier speeches against corruption in the Tolbert government seem to have saved her life. However, at the start of Doe's new era as president he again had Sirleaf charged with sedition, and she remained in prison for some seven months, being released in July 1986.

In the first months after being elected president, Doe killed thousands of people, adding yet another ethnic dimension to Liberia's woes by killing Gio people, of Quiwonkpa's ethnic group in Nimba County. With President Doe continuing his pressure on Sirleaf to take up her seat in the senate, it became clear that she had to leave if she wanted to stay alive. With the help of dear friends and colleagues, as Sirleaf recalls in her autobiography, she made it out of Liberia in 1986 by private plane, to Abidjan and then to the United States.

Once there, Sirleaf renewed her connections with the world of high finance, going to work as vice president and director of Equator Bank, of the Hong Kong and Shanghai Banking Corporation, in the Washington office. Living in Virginia, she watched from afar as Doe continued Liberia's slide into further disarray. This did not stop the Reagan government's support, however, and Secretary of State George Shultz stopped in Liberia on his tour of Africa in 1987. Like administration officials before him, Shultz supported Doe, if in somewhat muted terms, saying that Liberia could expect continued support from the United States but only if "Liberia is willing to help itself." Shultz ignored the fact that Doe arrested a group of protesters during Shultz's visit and that widespread political repression continued. The *New Liberian,* the Liberian government newspaper, was happy to describe the visit as "a demonstration of Republican President Reagan's reaffirmed commitment to support the Doe administration despite opposition in a Congress that is dominated by Democrats."[8] The *New York Times,* however, reported that "several Liberians, including a politician, a newspaper publisher and a human rights campaigner, said . . . that Mr. Shultz had made inaccurate statements . . . where he said Liberia had a free press, an elected Government and no political prisoners." Sirleaf was one of the people quoted by the *Times.* It said she was "'quite dismayed' by Mr. Shultz's portrayal of the Doe regime as an elected government and his appeal to opposition legislators. . . . And called Mr. Shultz's statements 'either deliberate misinformation or ignorance,' saying, 'The opposition stands by the position that the results of the 1985 election make the Government illegitimate.'"[9]

The end of the Cold War, signified by the fall of the Berlin Wall in 1989, diminished Liberia's importance to the United States. Doe thus became quite vulnerable. Charles Taylor had escaped from prison in the United

States in 1985, perhaps with the help of the CIA.[10] Testimony from Taylor's trial by the Special Court of Sierra Leone revealed that he had been in the employ of the CIA. Rumors had long abounded that it helped Taylor escape from the Boston jail in 1985, and although the CIA would not provide details, it confirmed that it worked with Taylor from the 1980s. Since then, Taylor had been marshaling forces to overthrow Doe and now began amassing troops to launch a military assault on Doe's government. Sirleaf had been working back in the States to garner opposition to Doe through founding the Association for Constitutional Democracy (ACDL) along with her colleague Professor Amos Sawyer and others. But in the face of a tyrant, simple politics was unlikely to work: Sirleaf turned to Charles Taylor.

As BBC correspondent Robin White says: "Charles Taylor's appeal was obvious. He was the complete opposite of Doe: Flamboyant, clever and well educated. And, above all, he could talk. . . . He was the 'Liberian Lip'; the 'Monrovian Motormouth.' He knew how to deal with the media."[11] Sirleaf claims that she had to at least try to work with the best available opponent of Doe, but Charles Taylor certainly came with lots of baggage. He had received military training as well as monetary backing from Muammar Gaddafi in Libya, who was spreading his money to develop his influence in North Africa and across the Sahara. On Christmas Eve 1989, Taylor declared war with an army of some 200 disaffected rebels. The war, now called the first Liberian Civil

War, lasted from 1989 to 1996, and killed more than 200,000 people. About a million people became internally displaced within Liberia, and some 700,000 people fled to Côte d'Ivoire, Ghana, Guinea, and Sierra Leone.[12] Taylor started his push in Nimba County, the county where Doe had massacred people after the 1985 election. Taylor then took control of key mining towns, which would generate profit to wage the final stages of war. At first it was thought the war would be swift, since Taylor was well armed and people wanted salvation from Doe. But Doe sent his army to wage a scorched-earth policy in Nimba, again killing Gio and Mano people whom he associated with the earlier coup. This made them much more inclined to join Taylor's army, which he called the National Patriotic Front of Liberia (NPFL).

With encouragement from the US State Department, Sirleaf and her colleagues in the ACDL collected and sent Taylor some $10,000 to help support his troops and to feed people in Nimba County. Later, Sirleaf decided to meet with Taylor. Sirleaf recalls in her biography that in May 1990, when Taylor was clearly a viable force, Sirleaf visited Taylor at his camp across the border from Côte d'Ivoire. She states that she walked, escorted by soldiers, to his camp, where she met Taylor, who was surrounded by heavily armed guards. Sirleaf wrote that she came away from the meeting with great reservations about Taylor's commitment to the good of Liberia. However, the next month, on June 19, 1990, Sirleaf gave a statement to the US House of Representatives' Foreign

Relations Subcommittee on Africa as an executive committee member of the Liberian Action Party (she was still employed as a vice president of Equator Bank). She talked of Doe's regime as a "political system which is maintained through state terrorism." She went on to say that the "uprising" (she did not mention Taylor by name in this context) should not be seen as a repeat of the coup of 1980 but rather as "an opportunity for creative transformation of the Liberian political landscape." In addition, Sirleaf said, "People, many of them children, have joined this struggle for freedom with little more than courage and hope for the future." And she continued, "The mandate must pass to Charles Taylor who must in turn commence the process toward democracy."[13] She pressured the US government to get Doe to resign and to make Taylor lay out a timetable for "free and fair elections." Records of Sirleaf's relationship with Taylor are contradictory and incomplete, but they raised enough questions that as we will see, she was later questioned by the Liberian Truth and Reconciliation Commission.

By July 1990, it had become clear that Taylor was no better than Doe, and possibly worse. Taylor killed people he considered a threat and coerced children to become killers, organizing a "Small Boys Unit." Sexual violence was ubiquitous among his armed forces. In the course of that summer, Liberia unraveled. One of the most infamous massacres of the time took place on July 31. Troops loyal to Doe killed hundreds of people who had sought refuge in St. Peter's Church in Sinkor, Monrovia.

A daily news chalkboard in Monrovia displays the latest headlines on the trial of former Liberian president Charles Taylor at the International Criminal Court in The Hague, the Netherlands. 2008. Photo by Lieutenant Colonel Terry VandenDolder, US AFRICOM.

Doe's ministers fled his government. Chaos descended on Liberia. A soldier, Prince Johnson, broke with Taylor and founded his own rebel movement, the Independent National Patriotic Front of Liberia (INPFL). Different factions fought to gain access to natural resources to fuel their wars, while conflict exacerbated existing ethnic tensions and created new ones. People fled their homes in rural areas in the face of advancing armies, and people fled Monrovia from the shelling and violence. In early August, in response to statements by Prince Johnson that he would begin rounding up Americans and other foreigners to force outside powers to intervene, the United States sent some two hundred marines to the capital to evacuate American citizens and dependents.[14]

The Economic Community of West African States (ECOWAS) stepped in to the breach, forming a mediating committee to try to draw up a peace plan. In addition, they created a new military force called the ECOWAS Monitoring Group (ECOMOG), which in late August 1990 sent some four thousand troops to Liberia to keep the peace. In the meantime the ECOWAS peace process (without Taylor's attendance) elected Amos Sawyer as the interim president. Although perhaps ECOMOG helped initially, over time the troops began to behave like the other militias, looting and pillaging their way across Monrovia. ECOMOG took sides, helping Prince Johnson once he broke from Taylor. They helped facilitate Johnson's capture of President Doe. Sirleaf was not in Monrovia when Prince Johnson's men tortured and murdered Samuel Doe. For the next year Amos Sawyer tried to govern while Johnson terrorized Monrovia and Taylor ruled the rest of the country. By the mid-1990s, Liberia was divided between the INPFL of Johnson, based in Monrovia, and Charles Taylor's "Greater Liberia" based in Gbarnga, in Bong County to the northwest.

Other armed groups also began to enter the fray, all increasingly using child soldiers as a way of boosting recruitment. As so often in the past, the armies raped and pillaged their way across Liberia, killing thousands, forcibly recruiting young boys into their militias and raping girls and then often turning them into sex slaves or "bush wives." The militias that emerged at this time included the United Liberation Movement of Liberia for Democracy (ULIMO), based in Sierra Leone and Guinea and made up of ex-soldiers who had fled in 1990; the Lofa Defense Force; and the Liberian Peace Council. Various groups broke up, often along ethnic lines, since both Doe and Taylor had mobilized in part around ethnicity. ULIMO, for example, divided into ULIMO-K (Kromah faction) affiliated with Mandingo and ULIMO-J (Johnson faction), which was dominated by Krahn.

Various groups made attempts to bring about peace. The Carter Center, founded by former President Jimmy Carter and concerned with human rights and democracy, opened an office in Monrovia in 1992 in an attempt to move Liberia toward peace. In September 1993, the UN established a small observer mission. Slowly, with many fits and starts, Liberia moved toward some kind of stability. Finally, in September 1995, the National Transitional Government of Liberia (the second) took power. But again militias fought over territory, minerals, and control over people. American citizens were evacuated as chaos descended again on Monrovia. It was estimated that 50 percent of Monrovia's population fled the capital looking for safety. Amos Sawyer, becoming an elder statesman for a constitutional vision, said, "The big three warlords . . . have decided they are going to crush whatever civilian opposition they can."[15]

Sirleaf watched these developments from afar in Washington, and then from Africa, where she was appointed director of the Regional Bureau for Africa of the United Nations Development Programme (UNDP) and thus assistant secretary-general of the United Nations. Thus as Taylor plundered the country's mineral resources to finance his campaign, Sirleaf temporarily disentangled herself from Liberian politics. Instead, she became involved in the politics of Africa generally at the very time that civil conflicts were breaking out across Africa as the USSR and United States turned away with the end of the Cold War.

The UNDP appointment gave Sirleaf an opportunity to expand her network to include the large international nongovernmental organizations (INGOs), which were increasingly dominating the world of development after the end of the Cold War. In her new role with UNDP, Sirleaf had the opportunity to work with people at the UN and to meet heads of state across the continent, including Julius Nyerere of Tanzania, whom she says she admired greatly, and Nelson Mandela, the newly elected president of a democratic South Africa and winner of the Nobel Peace Prize. Sirleaf chaired a number of big meetings, including one that tried to bring peace to Angola, which had been mired in civil war for many years.

Sirleaf was in charge of the Africa bureau when the Rwandan genocide occurred in the spring and summer of 1994. Eight hundred thousand people were killed in three months starting on April 4 as the Hutu Power government organized and facilitated the slaughter of people designated as Tutsis or Tutsi sympathizers. Along with other UN officials such as Kofi Annan, then

Monrovia. Map No. 3939, May 1996, United Nations.

secretary-general, Sirleaf bore witness but did not intervene. Sirleaf involved herself in efforts to aid Rwanda in the aftermath. In 1995, she headed a conference that raised about $700 million to help reconstruct Rwanda. Later, in 1998, she was a member of a seven-member committee that the Organisation of African Unity charged to investigate the genocide. The resulting report, published only in 2000, "Rwanda: The Preventable Genocide," took the international community to task for not getting involved and blamed France for standing by although they had thorough knowledge of everything.[16]

In Liberia, major fighting had broken out again in April 1996, which caused various foreign organizations, including the Carter Center, to leave Liberia. As a result, however, more and more pressure was put on the country, and on ECOWAS, to actually hold elections, even though they could only be imperfect in the context of war. Peace talks led to the August 1996 Abuja II peace deal, which set the stage for special elections. In 1997, Liberia finally had elections, and Sirleaf decided to run against Taylor, as part of a coalition between her old Liberian Action Party and others. She did this against the wishes of her family and in some respects against the pull of her career, which had her well placed to move up the administrative ladder at the United Nations. The divisions within Liberia replicated themselves within the coalition, and on arriving in Monrovia, Sirleaf found that the coalition had already approved another candidate. She returned to the United States but received a call from the Unity Party, previously a member of the coalition, to stand as their independent candidate. Twelve candidates were in the race, but the election really came down to Sirleaf and Charles Taylor.

With the slogan "Vote for Change" Sirleaf campaigned throughout the country, including down roads that were so muddy that cars could not travel. This way she came to be known in areas far from Monrovia and was reminded of the rural life with which she had become somewhat familiar in her youth. The Carter Center returned to Liberia to monitor the elections and set up the Liberia Election Project, opening its Monrovia office in April 1997. The center coordinated a forty-member international delegation of election observers, which affirmed that the elections were fair, if imperfect. The election did not go in Sirleaf's favor. The Carter Center's final report noted that although "the elections had some serious problems, including overwhelming advantage enjoyed by Charles Taylor in terms of resources, access to media, and organization, they still marked a critical step forward in consolidating peace." Sirleaf felt rather differently, because she saw that Taylor used various forms of intimidation, including having his helicopter flown low above the crowds that came to Unity Party rallies. Taylor's election slogan also intimidated voters with its reminder of the kind of violence he visited on people: "You killed my ma, you killed my pa: I will vote for you." Another voter reportedly said, "Charles Taylor spoiled this country, so he's the best man to fix it."[17]

With the somewhat muted endorsement of the election monitoring team, Charles Taylor was elected president of Liberia in 1997 with 75 percent of the vote. The preliminary statement from the Carter Center said, "In the face of tremendous challenges, the Liberian people have conducted a peaceful and orderly election, and turned out in high numbers to vote, and the collection and reporting of returns should lead to an accurate count." President Carter said that although the election was not exactly fair, since Taylor had so much more money and influence than his opponents, the election was not fraudulent. The preliminary statement from the center ended saying, "We hope the spirit of Election Day will guide Liberians in the days ahead." But this was not to be, at least not from Charles Taylor's perspective.

Taylor's rule, rather than ending the violence as people had hoped, only intensified the plunder of the country with the support of outside funders. According to Sirleaf, after the election, President Carter suggested it would be good if she were prepared to serve in Taylor's government. However, she rejected this proposal and returned to New York. She also says that Taylor reached out to her through one of his colleagues to offer her the position of head of the social security agency. She declined.[18] Taylor continued to try to silence opponents through assassinations and by accusing them of treason, a charge he also directed at Sirleaf in 1997. Nonetheless, Taylor received ongoing support from Gaddafi and from Pat Robertson, the American televangelist, who diverted planes meant for his humanitarian organization, Operation Blessing, to diamond mines in Liberia. In addition, in 1999 Taylor gave a government concession to Robertson's gold mining company, Freedom Gold Ltd., allegedly in return for generating support from the United States for Taylor's government.[19]

Sirleaf stayed away from Liberia but close enough to be keep a watch on developments. She moved to Côte d'Ivoire, then a jewel of economic stability. She set up a financial office using her contacts with Equator Bank from her first job in Washington. She established a venture capital firm for African investors called Kormah Development and Investment Corporation (Kodic). In the early months of Taylor's presidency, Sirleaf met with Taylor during visits back home. Answering the criticism that emerged during the Truth and Reconciliation Commission hearings, in her biography Sirleaf defends her meetings with Taylor, saying that she tried to offer him her experience, but that he was not open to her advice.[20]

In the late 1990s and early 2000s, peace was very far away. In 1999, two years after Charles Taylor's election as president of Liberia, civil war broke out again in Liberia, continuing to 2003, when warlords were forced to sign a peace agreement in Accra. Although there had been a brief lull in Liberia's conflict around the time of the elections, in April 1999, war began again. With the support of neighboring Guinea, soldiers calling themselves at that time the Organization of Displaced Liberians, referencing the terrible plight of refugees, entered Liberia in the northeastern county of Lofa. By June 1999, various groups united under the movement Liberians United for Reconciliation and Democracy (LURD). LURD soon proved to be the opposite of its name, and fighting renewed with Taylor's NPFL. Things were further complicated by the arrival of Revolutionary United Front fighters from Sierra Leone in support of Taylor, who also was deeply implicated in that civil war.[21]

Taylor accused Sirleaf of treason for supporting LURD because her name had been found on the body of a fighter. She rejected this angrily: "This is stupidity of the highest order. I have to conclude that the purpose of the accusation is a desperate attempt by Mr. Taylor to react to the report of his involvement in the Sierra Leone debacle and the fact that I have put out a press release on the 2nd of August calling for him to take action to clear his name and indicting him for his failure to respond to the needs of the Liberian people during the past three years."[22] Taylor's accusation that she had committed treason indicated that he perceived her as a continued threat, beyond her running against him in the election of 1997. In 2001 when he pardoned her and other leaders, she was interviewed to learn her response. She said, "Let me just say that people should not think that these actions by Mr. Taylor are coming because he's being magnanimous or he's being conciliatory. There is serious pressure on Mr. Taylor to do all the things he is doing now and more. The second point is that yesterday [August 2, 2001] was the fourth anniversary of Taylor's coming to power. He is in a big trouble and he put our country in big trouble—and he knows it. He knows that if he does not do something it is going to be worse for him."[23]

The international community increasingly was realizing the horror of the Taylor regime. By 2001 Taylor had basically demobilized the army and instead relied on armed units that owed their allegiance to him. One of the most important was the Anti-Terrorist Unit (ATU) made up of Liberians but also people from Burkina Faso and Gambia. Liberia slid further into violence. LURD artillery pummeled Monrovia, and roving bands of militia terrorized communities. The population of Monrovia swelled as people fled from the interior into the city. People who could do so left Liberia. In the 1980s, Liberia had 400 doctors, but by 2002, only about 30 remained.[24]

In Abidjan, Sirleaf continued practicing some of her key strengths: the desire and ability to network with people in positions of power to influence events in Liberia and to contribute to her standing. She met with leaders in the region to drum up support for peace and to isolate Taylor. In the early 2000s, Sirleaf became head of George Soros's Open Society Initiative for West Africa, OSIWA, which is committed to advancing democracy and the rule of law in the region. She visited with heads of state in the region to pressure them to give Taylor the cold shoulder. Sirleaf thus continued to be an important voice in the move to oust Taylor. A crisis group report from 2002, however, showed that lingering questions remained about Sirleaf's stature. It said that she was "one of the most prominent opposition figures" the West had supported in the election, but that she "finished second with a disappointingly low vote." The report concluded that although Sirleaf enjoyed name recognition in Monrovia, rural chiefs did not support her, and she was "widely criticized among the opposition as an early Taylor supporter, a charge she denies."[25] As I discuss in the next chapter, her early work with Taylor continued to shadow her presidency.

In the course of 2001, Taylor's intransigence finally became clear to the international community. He refused to attend a reconciliation conference at the end of 2001. Fighting intensified. In 2002, fighting drove tens of thousands of Liberians out of the country and into other areas of Liberia, where they became internally displaced people, and Taylor declared a state of emergency in the country. In March of the following year, rebel groups came within six miles or so of Monrovia and launched rockets into the capital. Two groups, the new Movement for Democracy in Liberia (MODEL) and LURD, now controlled much of the country. The ever-growing instability in Liberia, and anarchy in Monrovia, moved the United States also finally to distance itself from Taylor's presidency. Although it would take many months for that to become a reality, Taylor's time was coming to an end, and Sirleaf's time in the political spotlight was about to begin.

In June of 2003, President George W. Bush publicly stated that Taylor had to step down for the sake of peace. And to back up that statement, the United States sent over two thousand US Marines to wait off the Liberian coast. Taylor might have remained, but LURD was advancing on the capital. Nigeria offered Taylor asylum. Finally, both Taylor and the world began to move. On June 17 a ceasefire agreement was reached, and rebel leaders met in Ghana to begin peace talks, although hard fighting continued into July with rebels now in the capital and hundreds of people being killed. Negotiations to end the fighting started with ECOWAS agreeing to provide peacekeepers. On August 1, the United Nations Security Council adopted Resolution 1497 (2003), which authorized the establishment of a multinational force in Liberia and made provision for a "stabilization" force for Liberia to ensure peace. On August 11, 2003, Taylor resigned and left Liberia, handing over the government to a deputy, Moses Blah. Earlier that year, while still president, Taylor was indicted by the Sierra Leone special court. In 2012 he was found guilty in The Hague on eleven counts falling under war crimes, crimes against humanity, and recruiting child soldiers, a violation of international law. He was sentenced to fifty years in prison, an effective life sentence, which was upheld on appeal in September 2013. According to the *New York Times,* this made him the first head of state to be "convicted by an international court" since the Nuremberg trials after World War II.[26]

Meanwhile, in 2003, peace talks continued between various rebel factions and the government in Ghana. Sirleaf represented the Unity Party at the peace talks. The Accra Comprehensive Peace Agreement was signed on August 18, 2003. The agreement inaugurated a transitional government led by Gyude Bryant, a leader recognized as neutral, who governed Liberia until the general election was held in 2005. Sirleaf had been considered a front-runner for that post, but people loyal to Taylor saw her as too compromised, given her history of opposing him in the 1997 election, so Bryant was chosen for that role.[27] However, Sirleaf's time would come.

Women and Postconflict Liberia

The movement to peace was helped by the work of many Liberians working inside and outside Liberia. Liberian women's organizations were an instrumental part of the peace movement and later of the election of Ellen Johnson Sirleaf to the presidency in 2005. As noted, the early 2000s was also a time in which international human rights organizations and international multilateral organizations such as the UN put women's rights and women's roles in peacemaking on the agenda. Recognizing the failure of the international system to address the widespread rape of women in Bosnia Herzegovina and the Rwandan genocide, from the early 1990s to the early 2000s, the international community began to reassess its commitment to gender equality and women. Security Council Resolution 1325 on women, peace, and security, passed in 2000, was the first signal of this new awareness. It built on the work done by women in the 1990s in nongovernmental organizations (NGOs) from the Global South, and particularly Africa, to put women's rights on the agenda of international human rights.

Sirleaf was a key participant and shaper in this movement in the 2000s. In 2002 she coauthored with Elizabeth Rehn the document titled "Women, War, and Peace: The Independent Experts' Assessment on the Impact of Armed Conflict on Women and Women's Role in Peace," which established much of the framework for future discussions and policy about including women in peacebuilding. The authors traveled in 2001 and 2002 to fourteen countries around the world affected by conflict. They said, "In retrospect, we realize how little prepared we were for the enormity of it all: the staggering numbers of women in war who survived the brutality of rape, sexual exploitation, mutilation, torture and displacement. The unconscionable acts of depravity. And the wholesale exclusion of women from peace processes."[1] Many of the recommendations of the report have been implemented, if not always with the financial investment that would make them really powerful. In the years since, we have seen the creation of UN Women, the focus on gender equity in peacebuilding, and the development of indicators to assess the progress of gender mainstreaming.

In Liberia, as the film *Pray the Devil Back to Hell* and Leymah Gbowee's autobiography *Mighty Be Our Powers* document, women were deeply involved in the moves toward peace. As was her wont, Sirleaf worked within the system, sitting with the men at the table for peace negotiations. Other women helped in different and important ways to move Liberia toward peace.

Key organizations included Women in Peacebuilding Network (WIPNET) and Women of Liberia Mass Action for Peace (WLMAP), which met with Taylor and secured his promise to go to the peace talks. Gbowee, a leading voice in Liberia's WIPNET group and the leader of WLMAP, was awarded the Nobel Peace Prize, alongside Sirleaf and Tawakkol Karman of Yemen, in 2011 as a result of her work with that group.

WIPNET and others organized protests in Monrovia to show the rebels and the government that citizens were tired of war and desperate for peace. Supporters wore white to show their desire for peace. Women of different faiths and ethnicity united in the common cause for peace. With peace signed, the women of WIPNET became involved in demobilization. But as Gbowee writes: "A war of fourteen years doesn't just go away. . . . We had to confront the magnitude of what had happened to Liberia. Two hundred and fifty thousand people were dead, a quarter of them children. One in three were displaced. . . . One million people, mostly women and children, were at risk of malnutrition. . . . More than 75 percent of the country's physical infrastructure, our roads, hospitals and schools, had been destroyed."[2] Liberia faced a challenge indeed.

In August 2003, Sirleaf returned to Liberia after Charles Taylor was forced to leave the country. She came to participate in rebuilding the country. In the wake of her experience documenting the horrors experienced by women in war and their almost utter exclusion from postwar reconstruction, she was determined to put women's rights on the Liberian agenda. Sirleaf returned with so much expertise and so many international connections that she seemed almost predestined to be a leader of a post-Taylor Liberia. Marquette University gave Sirleaf an honorary degree in 2006, and the award notice succinctly summarized her deep connections to international finance as well as organizations working in development and for peace across Africa and beyond:

> Prior to her service as President, she served as Minister of Finance, President of the Liberia Bank for Economic Development and Investment, Vice President of Citicorp, Vice President of the HSBC Equator Bank, Senior Loan Officer of the World Bank, and founder and Chief Executive Officer of Kormah Development Corporation. She is also the founder of Measuagoon, a nonprofit organization that supports community development and education for girls. . . .
>
> Her Excellency was one of seven internationally eminent persons designated by the Organisation of African Unity to investigate the Rwanda genocide in 1999, one of five Commission Chairs for the Inter-Congolese Dialogue in 2002, one of the two international experts selected by the United Nations Development Fund for Women to investigate and report on the effect of conflict on women and women's roles in peace building in 2002, and Chairperson of the Open Society Initiative for West Africa from 2000 to 2003. She is a member of the Soros Foundation

Network and is also a Visiting Professor of Governance at the Ghana Institute of Management and Public Administration.[3]

Sirleaf's expertise in management, her connections to leading international organizations, and her history as an outspoken, if complicated, opponent of Taylor, made her an excellent candidate to work for the transition to peace. Acting president Bryant appointed her to head the Commission on Good Governance, a commission established by the Accra Peace Accord. The role of the commission was to create a climate of stability and transparency in government and "enable an environment which will attract private sector direct investment." The peace accord required that women be on the seven-member commission. This insistence that women be actual partners in peacemaking was in accordance with the mandate of Security Council Resolution 1325 of 2000. Liberia's transition to peace was thus one of the first peace processes to actively bring women into building the postconflict society.

Sirleaf's work with the commission and her goal of bringing professionalism to a decimated civil service, gave a hint of the style of her later presidency. Sirleaf is above all a bureaucrat who concentrates on management and structure. Grassroots organizing was the province of others, such as the women of the Women's NGO Secretariat of Liberia (WONGOSOL)—the grouping of NGOs focused on women's rights and experiences.

Many of these women were also instrumental in the peace process and continued to work for women's rights after the ending of the war. Sirleaf recognized the organizational excellence of the wider women's movement and the way that the movement had been able to reach new constituencies. Sirleaf held hearings around the country to alert people to the need for transparency in government. One of her accomplishments from that era, as she mentions in her autobiography, was to have the General Auditing Commission report to the legislature rather than to the president.[4]

In the years that followed in the lead-up to the 2005 election, many groups worked to ensure a democratic process that would put to rest the disastrous election of 1997. Building on alliances and agreements made in Accra, women tried to be involved in all aspects of peacebuilding in Liberia. This was easier said than done. UNIFEM and UNICEF worked with the women of WIPNET and other groups to translate the peace agreement into accessible language as well as to start various education initiatives. But as Gbowee recounts, the more formal processes involving the UN Mission to Liberia (UNMIL), such as disarmament, demobilization, and reintegration (DDR), remained focused on men and did not include women in decision-making capacities.[5]

But times were a-changing. Sirleaf resigned from the commission in order to run for the presidency, her second bid, having run in 1997. In the elections of 2005, Sirleaf emerged as a front-runner in a field of some initial twenty-two candidates. Sirleaf's success was due in part to her name recognition, which came from her long history in Liberian politics both inside and outside of the country. Sirleaf's success was also due to use of American-style electioneering techniques. She hired Willis Knuckles, one of her possible rivals, as her campaign manager. She raised money in the United States, where wealthier Liberians had moved during the war, through fund-raising events. And in Liberia, she used the rents from properties she owned (she was after all a successful businesswoman) to finance her campaign. Perhaps most important, as she describes in her autobiography, she hired Larry Gibson, a professor of law at the University of Maryland in the United States, who had been in the Carter administration, and had run Bill Clinton's campaign in Maryland in 1992. After traveling around Liberia, he ascertained that Sirleaf had a chance to win the election.[6]

Certainly, the country remained somewhat divided about Sirleaf's candidacy, reflecting long reservations about her early association with Taylor. But given the importance of women in forcing peace in Liberia, they were not going to let pass an opportunity to have an accomplished woman in the president's mansion. Sirleaf was thus fortunate to be able to count on the support of women in the vibrant peacebuilding community. They helped mobilize her campaign and took the word of the importance of voting far beyond Monrovia. Gbowee and other influential women such as Cerue Garlo, also of WIPNET, organized a campaign through UNMIL to register women to vote. Gbowee recalls that when they started the campaign some 15 percent of registered voters were women; by the end it was 51 percent. It was the high number of registered voters, and the enthusiasm of voters for the possibility of a female president that led Gibson to conclude that Sirleaf had a chance.

As Sirleaf recounts, Gibson helped structure a wise and disciplined campaign. A first principle was to avoid antagonizing opponents, whose support might well be needed later, as they indeed were in the runoff election. As Sirleaf writes in her autobiography, Gibson also understood the power of images: he had Sirleaf photographed in Western and Liberian dress, which could be used in different contexts. A-line skirts and jackets telegraphed Sirleaf's financial background and comfort dealing with international actors. Her long skirts and patterned blouses conveyed links to Liberia's indigenous communities. Also Sirleaf tended to appear without the traditional head wrap. In a country with high illiteracy it was important to develop symbols to telegraph larger meanings, including one's key approach to politics: Gibson decided that going without the head wrap signaled modernity, competency, and education, and would differentiate Sirleaf from other women candidates.[7]

Sirleaf's campaign also built on her expertise in communications and networking across boundaries. Although not a grassroots organizer herself, Sirleaf understood the importance of community mobilizing and the significance of acts, especially in a country where so many were illiterate. In the course of her campaign in 2005, she traveled to the fifteen counties of Liberia, thus making sure many people saw her. She in return saw how people lived and the ravages of the war; she heard firsthand of people's pain. What Sirleaf witnessed in the rural areas was very different from the life she had been living at the heights of international finance. By going out to the bush beyond Monrovia, her campaign demonstrated a new commitment to a unified Liberia. In the past, election campaigns had centered primarily on Monrovia. In a country historically divided between countryside and Monrovia, between indigenous and Americo-Liberian, between the poor and the elite, Sirleaf enacted a different vision for Liberia.

Running for president for the Unity Party, Sirleaf used all the tools at her disposal. She honed a message that focused on maternal images of care, her expertise as a financial manager and her education, her role as a longtime opposition figure, and her roots in both Americo-Liberian culture and indigenous Liberian society. Sirleaf turned the fact that she is a woman from a possible liability into a strength, aided much by the esteem in which Liberians now held the women who had done so much to urge peace. Sirleaf invoked ideas of the special gifts of women in restoring harmony and managing well. This resonated well in Liberia, which reeled from the posttraumatic stress of the war and which understands mothering as a central tenet of womanhood.

In the end, the election was really a two-person race. The leading contenders were George Weah, thirty-eight, a world-famous former soccer star, the only African to be voted FIFA international Footballer of the Year (in 1995), and Sirleaf, the consummate policy wonk. Weah was hugely popular in Liberia and probably the most famous Liberian outside the country at the time. He was initially expected to win the election. A *New York Times* report in August 2005 indicates the kind of enthusiasm generated by his candidacy: "Weah's soccer exploits, and his charitable work off the field, have made him a hero. . . . The day he announced he would run in the election . . . thousands of his fans danced in the streets of Monrovia. When Weah returned to Liberia this spring . . . his arrival shut down the capital for the day. As traffic snarled, businessmen shuttered their shops, and screaming students lined the road in from the airport. 'Weah in town,' they chanted. 'Politicians worry!'"[8]

Weah did win the first round of the elections, with Sirleaf trailing second. Voter turnout was high. Of the 1.35 million registered voters, 75 percent voted. As the United Nations stated, "The huge voter turnout was a rousing testimony to the people's desire for peace and an end to the cycle of violence and instability."[9] What Sirleaf and her team counted on was that in the end, Liberia would choose responsibility and education over star power. Weah had the latter in spades. He appealed to the youth. But Sirleaf had political and economic gravitas that included an MA from Harvard and years of working and networking in the world of politics and international development and finance. And she was a woman in a country where male leaders had proven irresponsible and where citizens saw that their female peers had helped bring peace. It was indeed now Sirleaf's time.

The runoff election was held on November 8, 2005. The women's vote really counted: more than half the registered voters in Liberia were women, thanks to the efforts of WIPNET and other groups who went all out to mobilize the female vote. Women were also a notable presence at campaign rallies and in general mobilizing. Through the streets of Monrovia they shouted the slogan and held signs saying, "Sirleaf—she's our man." This slogan captured both Sirleaf's unique presence in Liberian presidential politics, and indeed on the African continent, and also signified that she would be a strong ruler, just like a man. Sirleaf had enjoyed the moniker Iron Lady (a gesture to Margaret Thatcher's unique place in British politics) since her bid to oust Taylor in the 1997 election. An Iron Lady was what Liberia voted for.[10] Sirleaf won the runoff with some 60 percent of the vote. Weah submitted a complaint to the Supreme Court, but the election was ruled fair, albeit with some minor irregularities.

On November 23, 2005, Sirleaf was declared winner of the election. The world beyond Liberia that noticed, was thrilled. Politicians and leaders in the United States, who had found themselves uncomfortably on the wrong side of history in supporting Charles Taylor's

Daily Talk newsstand in Monrovia, reporting the policies of the incoming president, Ellen Johnson Sirleaf, in December 2005. Photo by Chris Guillebeau.

win in 1997, were effusive in their praise. The US House of Representatives congratulated Sirleaf on her presidential victory. In their statement they noted her many accomplishments; they said that with "her connections and legitimacy in the world of global finance and capital, [Ms. Sirleaf] stands a better chance of leading Liberia to economic recovery and international demarginalization."[11] It was more or less exactly on those principles, with a dose of feminism, that the new President Sirleaf began to organize her presidency. She was the first elected female president on the entire African continent. Just by being elected, Sirleaf made history. Now, she had to find a way to make her term as president also rewrite history in a good way.

The challenges Sirleaf faced were huge. Governor Lincoln Chafee of Rhode Island recalled in an interview that when he landed in Liberia during the election, his driver described the country, only two years out of war, as "this is where Mad Max meets the postapocalypse."[12] War-ravaged boys and young men, high on heroin and drunk with terror and bravado still roamed the streets. People tried to recover from histories of rape and abuse often far from their villages, which they had fled either in terror or shame, or both. The infrastructure of the country, never great to begin with, was devastated. Indeed, it hardly existed beyond the confines of Monrovia. In the city, which had had electricity in some neighborhoods, people had stolen the wires to sell. People lived on top of crumbling piles of bricks, the detritus of mortar shells and bullets all around. Old mansions, once glamorous, now were covered with grime, full of people with nowhere else to go. A whole generation had not gone to school, while children born at the beginning of the millennium would be able to go if only there were schools to go to. Liberia was an aching wound. After a shocking civil war, one could describe Liberia as a country with post-traumatic stress disorder.

It would take a miracle to make things better, and for a while it seemed a miracle had come in the form of Sirleaf. However, she is after all only human. Perhaps it would take more than drive and a particular kind of expertise to heal a country so depressed and mutilated by its histories of inequality and brutality.

President Sirleaf

On January 16, 2006, Ellen Johnson Sirleaf took the oath of office, thus becoming the twenty-third president of Liberia. People thronged the streets of Liberia in celebration. Representatives of countries from around the world attended the inauguration. These included Condoleezza Rice, the US Secretary of State, as well as leaders such as Thabo Mbeki, then president of South Africa. Sirleaf gave a rousing speech, talking of the need for economic development, an end to corruption, and the need for good governance, reconciliation, and responsibility. She particularly noted the contributions of women to ending the civil war. And she pledged, right then, to "give Liberian women prominence in all affairs of our country. My Administration shall empower Liberian women in all areas of our national life."[1]

Liberia and Sirleaf faced overwhelming challenges. In 2006, Liberia had 3.4 million people. With a per capita income of just over $100, Liberia was one of the world's poorest nations. The country had virtually no income apart from that flowing from the concessions to foreign companies, including Firestone. But those concessions

President Ellen Johnson Sirleaf waves to the audience at her inauguration in Monrovia, January 16, 2006. White House photo by Shealah Craighead.

also drained Liberia of the income that could be generated if the country managed its own vast natural resources rather than outsourcing the labor, and thus most of the profits. And how was Sirleaf to get the country on the move, with such a high illiteracy rate, some 80 percent, given the war and earlier discrimination? How to knit together a country with some sixteen indigenous languages, a common history only of war and exploitation, and now with hundreds of thousands of people needing sustenance and comfort who had been forced from their homes during the war. With people's life expectancy only forty-seven years, there was no time to waste. And how to return faith in the very idea of government in a country in which the government had mostly been about plundering the interior for taxes and rubber while creating a settler haven in Monrovia? What a legacy of war. As Sirleaf said in her address to the joint session of the US Congress after she became president:

> Our children are dying of curable diseases— tuberculosis, dysentery, measles, malaria. Schools lack books, equipment, teachers and buildings. The telecommunications age have passed us by.
>
> We have a $3.5 billion external debt, lent in large measures to some of my predecessors, who were known to be irresponsible, unaccountable, unrepresentative and corrupt. The reality that we have lost our international creditworthiness bars us from further loans, although now we would use them wisely.
>
> Our abundant natural resources have been diverted by criminal conspiracies for private gain. International sanctions imposed for the best of reasons still prevent us from exporting our raw materials. Roads and bridges have disappeared or been bombed or washed away. We know that trouble once again could breed outside our borders. The physical and spiritual scars of war are deep indeed.[2]

One of Sirleaf's first tasks was to try to get the government up and running in a way that aligned with her vision of good, responsible governance. Sirleaf brought much talent and insight to the task of rebuilding a postconflict country. She recognized the importance of including former opponents in this huge mission of rebuilding Liberia. Although George Weah declined her offer of a government position, other leaders did come on board. But, as she describes in her autobiography, the challenges were huge. Some of the people she would like to have included in government did not have the qualifications she thought essential. Ministers had to work in offices that had been stripped of furniture, with no electricity, no bathrooms, no way of actually working. In addition, as Sirleaf lamented: "One of the most difficult challenges—one of the toughest things in Liberian culture in general—is simply creating the capacity to get things done. . . . This is one of our greatest challenges: developing the capacity of our own people to do all the jobs a functioning democracy requires."[3]

Liberia clearly was going to need outside help both in terms of expertise to get public institutions up and running and to rebuild the infrastructure. The United Nations (UN) was the key partner. The United Nations continued its work through the UN Mission in Liberia (UNMIL) and sixteen other programs, agencies, and the World Bank. UNMIL worked hard to restore Liberia from the earliest days of peace through Sirleaf's presidency. By June 2007 some 314,000 internally displaced people had been returned home through the work of the UN Refugee Agency (UNHCR) and others.[4] By 2007, at the close of the voluntary repatriation program, UNMIL had helped 105,000 refugees return to Liberia.[5] In 2013, UNMIL was still providing stability, security, and expertise in policing, retraining of military units, and running of a government, with the force reduced to some 7,500 from the original 15,000 in 2003. From 2004 to 2007, the UN Police, UNPOL, trained and deployed 3,500 Liberia National Police (LNP) officers; most were stationed in Monrovia, but by the end of 2007 UNPOL had deployed 1,200 LNP officers to the countryside.[6] In addition, UNMIL helped train the army. UNMIL also included a senior gender adviser with staff support, to help mainstream gender equity into the new government and develop relations with civil society. As a sign of the new UN commitment to gender equality, women also served as peacekeepers, with women from Nigeria coming first in 2003. Since 2007, women peacekeepers from India have guarded the presidential mansion. UNMIL also helped build schools across Liberia.

In addition Sirleaf turned to the many Liberians who had moved overseas during the civil war. These included the elites who could afford to go in the first wave of emigration in the early 1990s, as well as those who fled any way they could as Taylor unleashed his tyranny later in that decade. Liberians in Ghana, Atlanta, Minnesota, New York, and London returned home with enthusiasm. People returned from middle-class lives abroad and from refugee camps in neighboring countries. They brought with them different skills, connections, and levels of financial investments, but all brought acumen. They could help rebuild Liberia. Dr. Elizabeth Davis-Russell, formerly provost at SUNY Cortland, came home to lead Tubman University in Harper, in the far south county of Maryland. Yar Donlah Gonway-Gono returned with a PhD to start a community college in her home county, Nimba. Two years after Sirleaf's inauguration, the changes the Diaspora was making to the country and especially to Monrovia were clear. In Congo town, the old suburb of the elites, people built big houses that dwarfed their poorer neighbors. People from the Diaspora eagerly set up restaurants, filling stations, and businesses, in the hope that Liberia would rise again as a tourist destination for the African American community, as it had been in the 1970s. People also joined the government and headed educational institutions. But other people in the Diaspora remained afraid of returning to Liberia, not entirely convinced that the war was in the past. Charles Taylor had contributed to great violence across the region, destabilizing Sierra Leone, Guinea, and Côte d'Ivoire. People feared that hostilities could easily reopen. And stringent citizenship rules that prevent Liberians from holding dual passports and which allow only Liberian nationals to own property continued to cause resentment and unease.

Sirleaf turned to her wide network created over the thirty-five years of working in international finance and local politics. She relied on personal ties and on the optimism the world felt that with her at the helm, Liberia would flourish. As she said in an interview in 2013, "I bring to the international development debate many years of experience in the private sector and the public sector, working internationally and at home. . . . I'm able to represent Liberia effectively; I'm able to speak convincingly."[7] Sirleaf spoke in the language of international capital and development that the people with funding could understand. As a result, foreign aid in all its dimensions helped pull Liberia from the pit created by war and earlier histories. The United States became a key government partner. In the two years after the peace accord, the United States gave some $880 million to Liberia, including more than $520 million to UNMIL. The United States also gave $90 million to help refugees and internally displaced persons. In the first year of Sirleaf's term, the United States committed itself to $270 million.

During Sirleaf's first term, Liberia became in effect Development Central. Liberia offered a laboratory for international development experts who were struggling to find new ways of partnering. In the late 1990s and early 2000s, the international community was still reeling from failures to stop violence and create peace in the former Yugoslavia, Rwanda, and the Democratic Republic of Congo. As we have seen, this soul-searching led to Security Council Resolution 1325 of 2000, which emphasized the need for women to participate in peacebuilding and postconflict reconstruction. It also led to a new emphasis on partnering and good governance as central pillars of development practice. Now, with a feminist president possessing unusual financial and administrative skills, development experts saw in Liberia an opportunity to do good.

International aid organizations such as Doctors without Borders, CARE, and the Carter Center sent experts to staff hospitals and clinics. These organizations also developed and provided training on the rule of law and on how to end gender-based violence. In addition, they helped run parts of the government. Sirleaf faced a dilemma: if she did not use the help of outsiders, she could not run her government, but by relying so much on foreigners, she risked alienating her citizenry.

Women's Council, National Council of Elders and Chiefs at International Women's Day, Monrovia. March 2008. Photo by Institute for Developing Nations, Emory University.

The term "lacking capacity" became a mantra of development experts and the government. It was not one necessarily appreciated by Liberian citizens who had had the capacity to survive numerous corrupt regimes and the brutality of civil war and were still standing. The issue of what kind of capacity Liberia needed remained a simmering issue of debate in Monrovia, one that rose again in the Ebola outbreak of 2014.

Sirleaf also fulfilled her commitment to women's rights and to honor the contributions of women to building peace in Liberia. She reinvigorated the Ministry of Gender and Development, established under Taylor in 2001. The ministry now was tasked with overseeing the huge transformations she wanted to bring about in women's rights. The revised rape law, passed by the parliament just prior to her inauguration, was a key piece of legislation invoked by the Sirleaf administration to emphasize its commitment to ending impunity for sexualized violence. As in the road to peace, women's groups were instrumental in the passage of the law.[8] The new rape law expanded the definition of rape by using gender-neutral language, which acknowledges men also can be victims of sexualized violence. The law expanded forms of rape to include gang rape, rape with a weapon, and rape of minors. In addition, rape was made a felony, and thus it could not be bargained away through negotiation between parties or their representatives. This was often done in rural areas, where police were, and still are, virtually absent, and where women are loath to bring charges of rape against men for fear of community reprisals. Thus, for the rape law to have teeth, other things needed to be done. The Association of Female Lawyers of Liberia (AFELL) was instrumental in the creation of a new court to handle cases of gender-based violence. This Criminal Court E is supposed to ensure attention to handling and resolving rape cases. However, there is a great backlog of cases, and an initial study of the workings of the court suggested that many structural impediments remain to its effective functioning.[9]

But governance was only one of a host of factors that would rebuild Liberia. As part of the peace settlement in Accra, warlords had agreed that Liberia have a truth and reconciliation commission of the kind that had been instituted in South Africa after its democratic elections in 1994. Liberia's transitional government legally created the Truth and Reconciliation Commission of Liberia (TRC) on May 12, 2005. The mandate of the Liberian TRC was "to promote national peace, security, unity and reconciliation." It was charged with investigating some twenty years of civil war between January 1979 and October 14, 2003, that is, events around the coup led by Samuel Doe, to the end of the Liberian Civil War. The TRC was tasked with identifying the root causes of the war, documenting human rights abuses, creating opportunities for victims and perpetrators to engage in dialogue toward reconciliation, identifying economic crimes, paying special attention to women and children, and writing a report to the government giving recommendations for criminal prosecution and amnesty.[10] The government put some $7 million toward the TRC, and Sirleaf inaugurated the commissioners shortly after her inauguration, thus setting in motion the TRC. She also made public efforts to encourage citizens to engage with the TRC, visiting the commission in July 2007, for example, as well as issuing statements urging people to participate.

In many ways, the Liberian TRC was a model truth commission, coming after a decade in which transitional justice mechanisms of this sort had become institutionalized in peacebuilding efforts. The TRC did a lot of hard work, taking over 22,000 statements, 500 live statements to hearings of the TRC, holding a national conference on reconciliation, and meeting with regional leaders. The Liberian TRC was the first to have a TRC also for the Diaspora, to make sure that the Liberians living outside the country had a voice in the reconciliation process. The Liberian TRC was a pioneer in its attention to sexual violence and the experience of women and children; it was very intentional about gender equity.

Learning from the South African experience, which had sidelined women, the Liberian TRC made sure to include women on the commission: of the ten commissioners, four were women. The journalist Massa Washington headed the Gender Committee, which investigated crimes against women. Extensive conversations and workshops with women around the country gave granular detail to the documentation of sexual violence:

the report concluded that all parties to the conflict engaged in rape and other forms of sexual violence. The number of women affected by sexual violence is hard to judge, as there is a wide variation in numbers cited in different reports. A World Health Organization study reported that out of 412 female respondents, 77 percent experienced rape during the civil wars.[11] The Liberian TRC reported that only some 8 percent of violations reported involved sexual violence, although of course the number reported and what people actually experience diverge. In any event, the TRC report stated that because of their sex, "women and girls experienced incredible acts of violence and torture. On account of their gender, women and girls were subjected to abduction, slavery, and forced labor." The Liberian TRC thus brought into view women's experiences and was thus aligned with some of the goals of the Sirleaf administration: to lift up women and include them in Liberia's social and body politic.

However, the Liberian TRC was plagued from the start by divisions between commissioners and a sense that it was foisted upon the country instead of arising from a genuine desire by participants to heal the wounds of the past. The TRC did not interview Charles Taylor, who was then on trial at The Hague for his crimes in connection with the civil war in Sierra Leone. Thus a key figure in the carnage unleashed on Liberia did not participate, which some felt limited the possibilities of reconciliation. In addition, Liberians saw few results from the work and money spent on the TRC. Old wounds were reopened, with little sense that the wounds would be healed.

For Sirleaf, the TRC process was a difficult time. A witness to the TRC claimed that he saw Sirleaf in military uniform in 1990, the suggestion being that Sirleaf was more involved than she acknowledges in her autobiography.[12] Although Sirleaf acknowledges meeting Taylor in the bush, she insists that the meeting was in a personal capacity only and that shortly thereafter she severed the connection.[13] The TRC decided to call Sirleaf to appear because of her earlier public ties to Charles Taylor. In February 2009, President Sirleaf appeared before the TRC in Monrovia as part of its "institutional and thematic hearing on economic crimes." In her statement she said that she had given assistance to Taylor, but this was before she and the general public realized that he was a war criminal. Sirleaf also vigorously denied charges that she had appeared in a military uniform: "I have never worn a military uniform in my life. If anyone can say that, then I will go to my travel documents and disprove them. I think it was a case of mistaken identity."[14]

In order to present the final report to the country, the Liberian TRC organized a National Conference of Reconciliation from June 15 to June 20, 2009, at the Unity Conference Center built by the original Organisation of African Unity, outside of Monrovia. The conference acknowledged the historic inequalities between Americo-Liberians, or Congo, and indigenous

Liberians, as well as the disrespect created by features of the national imaginary. The memorandum of the conference stated that the motto of Liberia "The Love of Liberty Brought Us Here," in which Liberians and settlers were clearly conflated, should be changed. Instead, the conference recommended that the motto read "The Love of Liberty Unites Us Here." This is a change that has not been made. One wonders why, given that it would be a hugely symbolic gesture of reconciliation.

The final Liberian TRC report was delivered to parliament in June 2009. Revised volumes 1 and 3, which included appendixes and specific reports, were released in December 2009. The report is both a fairly scholarly accounting of the histories of abuses, violence, and inequality in Liberia and, in the context of the time, a bombshell. The report recommended that the leaders of the various warring factions, including Charles Taylor, be prosecuted. That was expected. But in addition, on page 361 of volume 2, the report identified people "subject to/recommended for public sanctions." The report recommended that these people be "barred from holding public office, elected or appointed, for a period of thirty (30) years." The report named names, and one of those names was Ellen Johnson Sirleaf.

As Lansana Gberie, a former head of the International Center for Transitional Justice in Liberia at the time, argues, this was an extraordinary claim. Lustration, the censoring of officials from engaging in public life, is usually reserved for people who abused their official positions. Sirleaf was not charged with that. In addition, Sirleaf after all was imprisoned by Samuel Doe for a year. The charges against Sirleaf, whom the report mentions only a few times, are about her meeting with Taylor, in whose government she never served.

Despite her disagreement with this section of the report, Sirleaf publicly proclaimed her support for the TRC process. In an interview in May 2010, she said that the commission had done "a good job trying to examine the root causes of our nation's conflict and they've made some very useful suggestions and recommendations about how we go about with the healing process."[15] However, she said that the lustration clause, which bans people from holding public office, and in the case of Liberia, often when they had had no chance to appear before the commission, raised concerns about due process. Sirleaf clearly disagreed with the report: she ran for a second term as president, in clear opposition to this recommendation of the Liberian TRC.

In her second campaign for president in 2011, Sirleaf was no longer the peaceful yet strong heroine. Now she was a sitting president, responsible for all that had happened and had not been accomplished in her first term, and with the TRC recommendation casting a long shadow. In contrast to the great support for her in her first election campaign, now popular opinion generally went the other way. As Prue Clarke and Emily Schmall reported at the time of Sirleaf's reelection campaign:

As she runs for a second term as president, the 72-year-old Johnson Sirleaf has been booed and heckled. Her first term has been one long cascade of corruption scandals, and critics of her administration say they've been attacked, intimidated, and offered bribes. No one accuses the president of being personally responsible for any of these abuses, but she has clearly been let down badly by many people she trusted. In fact, although Liberia has no credible opinion surveys to predict the election's outcome, many political analysts believe Johnson Sirleaf could lose, particularly if balloting goes to a second round after the Oct. 11 vote. Some Liberians have actually threatened violence if she's reelected.[16]

Despite concern that she would not win, the country voted for Sirleaf a second time. Her compatriots voted in the shadow of her winning the Nobel Peace Prize, awarded on October 7, just days before the election. Inside Liberia, some saw the prize as a show of force by the international community worried that Sirleaf would not win a second term. Winston Tubman, Sirleaf's main rival, and the nephew of President William Tubman, who had ruled Liberia from 1944 to his death in 1971, lamented, "On the eve of the election the Nobel Peace Prize committee gives her this prize, which we think is a provocative intervention within our politics."[17]

The election was held in October, and with no clear winner, a runoff election was slated to be held between

Sirleaf and Winston Tubman. Various election bodies, including the Carter Center, affirmed that the election met the required standards of freedom and transparency. But on November 4, Winston Tubman boycotted the runoff elections, thus leaving Sirleaf as the only candidate. Tubman argued that the members of the National Election Commission needed to be replaced in order for unbiased elections to proceed, given allegations of voting irregularities. Subsequent clashes occurred between members of his party, the Congress for Democratic Change, and the Liberian national police. The bitterness left by the Liberian TRC lingered. Former warlord Prince Johnson, now a twice-elected senator, threw his weight behind Sirleaf because Tubman's party had endorsed the recommendation that Johnson be prosecuted for war crimes. On November 8, 2011, Liberians again went to the polls, with a 61 percent turnout. Sirleaf emerged victorious with 90 percent of the vote.

Conclusion

From the time of her first ascendancy to the Liberian presidency, Ellen Johnson Sirleaf enjoyed great acclaim from countries and organizations around the world. In her role as president of Liberia, a country that became the model for postconflict reconstruction, Sirleaf achieved high visibility. In addition, world leaders recognized her for her historic leadership across various important spheres from politics to finance to women's rights. The Nobel Peace Prize of 2011 thus was part of a broader recognition for all that Sirleaf brought to the post–Cold War world.

However, while Sirleaf's star rose in the international arena, her government's reliance on international expertise created distrust between citizens and government, a distrust that grew in her second term. Many Liberians had become hostile to Sirleaf, but the West, enamored of her, could not see this. The year after she won the Nobel Prize, the former chairman of the Liberian Truth and Reconciliation Committee, Jerome J. Verdier, issued a blistering critique of Sirleaf, accusing her of presiding over a corrupt regime. This was a view shared by many. In 2013, a new public think tank, the Liberia Institute of Public Integrity, noted in its inaugural policy paper that there was US$2.01 billion in aid that could not be accounted for.[1]

The president's reliance on her family members stoked accusations of nepotism. A person close to the president argues that Sirleaf ended up relying on her sons because she had become disillusioned by corruption she could not control and had reason to fear for her life. Nonetheless, the high-profile positions of three of her sons, as well as internal disputes between them, fed fires of dissatisfaction with Sirleaf's second term. Her eldest son, James T. Sirleaf, worked for First International Bank. Charles is the deputy governor for operations of the Central Bank of Liberia. Rob, the son who refused to remain behind when Ellen went to Washington, became involved in Liberia raising money for soccer fields, working with the Robert Johnson Foundation, and focusing on Liberian youth. Rob became chairman of the National Oil Company of Liberia and promised to clear it of corruption. He did not take a salary. He then took over First National Bank, and that is when he appears to have come into conflict with his elder brother James, whom he fired. In December 2014 Robert Sirleaf ran for the senate, a move that fueled accusations that Ellen Johnson Sirleaf was building a political dynasty.[2] He was roundly trounced in that senate race by none other than George Weah, the famous soccer star who had opposed Sirleaf in the first election. Weah won his senate seat with 78 percent of the vote.[3] In October 2014, the Liberian justice minister resigned, charging the president with blocking an investigation into corruption in the National Security Agency, run by her ex-husband's son Fumba Sirleaf.[4]

Sirleaf is no angel, nor a saint. She is in a sense a missionary for a different idea of government, a technocratic one staffed by people educated in finance, management, and administration—in fact, her own type of training. She continues to see this type of governance as the form required. In a 2010 interview with the Council on Foreign Relations, she said as much: The problem is of "capacity at all levels in the society, in government, as well as in civil society. So the biggest thing is, do you have the expertise to be able to put all these people to work."[5]

Through her second term, Sirleaf continued to enjoy the support of the international community. Perhaps this was because she was legible to them in a way that she was not necessarily to all of her fellow Liberians. The language she spoke, of administration, capacity, finance, and governance, matched well and had in some sense informed the new development era with its emphasis on governance, indicators, and assessment. As of 2013, she had received a vast number of international awards. In 2007, Sirleaf received the Presidential Medal of Freedom, the highest honor awarded to civilians by the US President. In 2012 France also bestowed its highest honor, the Grand Croix of the Légion d'Honneur, and in the same year, Sirleaf received the Indira Gandhi Prize for Peace, Disarmament and Development.

President Ellen Johnson Sirleaf and US Secretary of State Hillary Rodham Clinton at the US Department of State in Washington, DC, April 21, 2009. State Department photo.

She received at least seventeen honorary degrees from institutions such as Harvard, Spelman, and Yale. She also continued to work at the highest levels of international peacebuilding and finance. In 2013 she became the chairperson of the African Peer Review Mechanism. And African heads of state and the African Union chose her to head a committee to chart the postmillennium goals agenda. In 2012 Forbes ranked her among the world's one hundred most powerful women.

But at home, things were beginning to become complicated. The terrible outbreak of Ebola in 2014 exposed the longevity of the incredible challenges that had faced Sirleaf when she first took office. So much of what challenged Liberia in 2006 remained in 2014: the weak infrastructure, corruption, and distrust of government.

Ironically, the fact that so much money had been spent on rebuilding Liberia exacerbated citizens' dissatisfaction. As of 2010, for example, Liberia was the third-largest recipient of US aid in the entire continent. But in 2014, 71 percent of the population lived on less than a dollar a day, and basic sanitation was available only to the wealthy, and mainly in Monrovia. And sexual violence against women remained an open national wound. In 2013, 65 percent of the 1,002 reported cases involved victims who were only three to fourteen years of age. Yet only 137 cases came to court, and only 49 rapists were convicted.[6] An Amnesty International report in 2011 showed the challenges in prosecuting rape, with magistrates taking up cases not actually under their purview, too few social workers to take care of survivors, and the difficulty of even getting the accused to court because of the shortage of transportation.[7]

Sirleaf had certainly tried. As Blair Glencorse, chair of Accountability Lab, an anticorruption NGO in Liberia, wrote in 2013, Sirleaf had done much to create transparency in government by passing a Freedom of Information Act. And she had wrested more control over Liberia's natural resources and tried to stem corruption. However, as Glencorse also noted, Sirleaf herself said in 2012 that corruption in Liberia remained "systemic and endemic."[8] In addition, the promise of securing profit from companies' investment in Liberia's natural resources has faded. A "legal loophole" allows the government to issue Private Use Permits to companies:

sixty-six such permits have been issued. These permits often apply to collectively owned community lands, and provide less revenue to the government than other contracts.[9] In addition, questions about Sirleaf's relationship with Taylor remained. And citizens continued to complain about Sirleaf's refusal to comply with the recommendations of the Liberian TRC. In May 2014, for example, Bernard Gbayee Goah, president of an organization called Operation We Care for Liberia, an activist blog dedicated to the "complete transformation of Liberia," criticized Sirleaf for not heeding the recommendation of the TRC and stepping down. "Ellen Johnson-Sirleaf is not capable of navigating her own people through the rough waters of justice because doing so would mean holding herself accountable."[10]

But how much could one ask of a single person? Among many accomplishments, we can note that she reduced Liberia's crippling international debt, brought running water and electricity to Monrovia, and in partnership with other countries and companies constructed roads across the country, which will help unify Liberia as well as stimulate commerce. She had the international trade sanctions (imposed against Charles Taylor) lifted, and she provided free education up to the ninth grade. In 2006, Sirleaf launched the Girls' National Education Policy, in cooperation with UNICEF, which dramatically increased opportunities for girls to be educated, and her government also partnered with USAID to increase girls' education.

In an extended interview in July 2013, President Sirleaf answered questions about corruption in her government, her numerous trips abroad, and the slow pace of change in Liberia put to her by Darryl Ambrose Nmah, director general of the Liberian Broadcasting System. An apparently frustrated Sirleaf patiently answered questions, returning again and again to the challenges Liberia faced after the war. She said that a primary problem was the capacity of Liberians to enact the change and the governance that was required. She defended her trips abroad, saying that these helped give Liberia a voice in the world and brought investment to Liberia. She spoke to a record of dismissing people in her government for corruption, and she pointed out how in trying to be democratic, and being sensitive to communities' perspectives, some investments that would have brought more employment had taken much longer to get off the ground. Sirleaf concluded the interview with her perspective on Firestone, the company to which the Liberian government had ceded so much power back in 1926. In some ways, one could see this as exemplary of what Sirleaf's approach had sought to accomplish: through working with powerful companies, which brought employment opportunities and foreign capital to Liberia, she believed change could happen:

> We have to work with the concessions. I'll give you the example of Firestone. You remember where the people used to live? That's part of the investment. They used

to live in hovels. We said to Firestone, you've got to give us a five-year plan to transform that Plantation and get better living conditions for the workers. Go to Firestone today; see the transformation that's taking place there. Today, Firestone students are the ones that are making the highest in the WAEC Exams. LAC will follow; Salala will follow the same pattern; COCOPA will follow. Any other rubber or agriculture concession will do the Firestone model. Those are part of the investment rewards that are taking place, that people say they don't see there. The other day, Firestone workers just completed their Collective Bargaining Agreement in which their wages were raised. They used to carry the rubber on their shoulders; that has changed now; they have to have little trailers where they can now put the container on the trailer. Those are the good things that are happening, but you know, people don't see that one. Please come with me in the countryside sometimes, so they can see what's happening outside. People always say Monrovia is not Liberia, and they're correct. Out of 4 million people, 1.5 million people are right here in Monrovia. They are making Monrovia Liberia. We are trying to make Liberia Liberia by doing things out there, so that we create the jobs out there, so people can live out there.[11]

Perhaps the challenges facing the president were just too many, coming too fast, and the legacy of some 160 years of gross inequality was just overwhelming. So by the time

Ebola hit in 2014, many citizens had come to feel that Sirleaf had done little to change conditions for Liberians.

A hemorrhagic fever with a very high death rate, 40–90 percent, and with no known cure at the time, Ebola started in Guinea and moved quickly to Sierra Leone and Liberia. The first case in Liberia occurred in northern Lofa County, the county where LURD had launched its war on Charles Taylor. Lofa is a heavily forested county bordering on Guinea and Sierra Leone where people walk back and forth across the borders visiting family and trading. The first case of Ebola was found in March 2014 in a patient who had returned from Guinea. Previous Ebola outbreaks had happened in relatively isolated environments in central Africa and had been contained. Thus, for a while, authorities did not worry much about containment. However, by June 2014, Ebola had continued to spread. By August, Ebola was in Monrovia. The coming of Ebola to a heavily populated city changed the dynamics of Ebola completely, turning it from a deadly disease that could be contained to one that threatened to ruin the three countries in which it was now spreading.

On August 7, 2014, Sirleaf declared a state of emergency. This empowered the government to suspend civil liberties as it saw necessary. Sirleaf said that she had enacted "extraordinary measures for the very survival of our state and for the protection of the lives of our people."[12] Ebola now exposed the degree of animosity that poorer citizens still harbored against government.

People were skeptical that Ebola really was contagious and blamed Sirleaf for just trying to bring more development dollars into government pockets. People said things like: "Sirleaf . . . and her minister of health want to pocket money so they have come up with a new tactic to collect money and share."[13] In West Point, a crowded informal settlement in Monrovia, citizens entered an Ebola containment center, freeing patients and taking mattresses and other materials. The government soon placed West Point under quarantine, with the police and the Liberian army patrolling. A military blockade prevented people from Bomi and Grand Cape Mount counties from entering Monrovia.

By late August, the Centers for Disease Control and Prevention in the United States was declaring the Ebola outbreak in Liberia the worst the world has ever seen. The head of the CDC praised ordinary Liberians for trying: "I have been impressed by the response I have seen. We met dozens of volunteers answering dozens of calls every day, 24 hours daily, we met dozens of healthcare workers and dozens of community volunteers in rural areas willing to help with the response."[14] But the reality was that Liberia's infrastructure, neglected for decades, damaged by war, and only just recovering, could not cope with Ebola. Soon doctors and other health workers treating patients died, as did many of the patients they treated. Without basic medical supplies such as latex gloves, good sanitation in hospitals, and a healthy government infrastructure, Liberia became ground zero for the disease.

Again, Sirleaf's relationships built up over so many years came to Liberia's rescue. She appealed to the United States to help her crippled country fight the disease. The United States, always wary of getting too involved in Liberia, woke up to the seriousness of Ebola. In September, the US military inaugurated "Operation United Assistance" to coordinate the military's response to Ebola in Liberia. President Obama authorized three thousand troops to be sent to Liberia to help with logistics and nonmedical help. By early November the military had set up a field hospital for infected health care workers and a hundred-bed hospital. The Cuban and Chinese governments also sent doctors and other personnel to help stem Ebola. By November, the CDC noted that cases of Ebola were beginning to decline in Liberia, but the epidemic raged on in neighboring Sierra Leone and Guinea.[15] Time will tell if Ebola becomes a scary chapter in the history of Liberia or a major theme of its future. But by April 2015, Liberia became the first country in the Ebola-affected region to have no new case of Ebola. The last confirmed death from Ebola occurred November 24, 2015.

One of the reasons for the containment of Ebola in Liberia was the move by communities to work toward safer burial practices, which stopped the spread of the disease. Liberians also embraced the campaign to wash hands with bleach and to stop greeting one another with the traditional Liberian handshake, at least for a time. In addition, there was a concerted effort by government and civil society actors to reach out to communities through radio and advertisements, with the government helping to produce a hip-hop song titled "Ebola Is Real." George Weah and the Ghanaian musician Sydney produced a song about Ebola in 2014 to raise awareness.[16] In March 2015, President Sirleaf acknowledged that she had made some errors in her first reactions to the epidemic, particularly with regard to her declaration of a state of emergency. She said that in hindsight sealing off West Point had "created more tension in the society" and promoted distrust between citizens and their government.[17]

When running for president a second time, Sirleaf said she had underestimated the challenges facing her country. She lamented: "We found a totally collapsed economy, dysfunctional institutions, lack of proper laws and policies, low capacity, and a value system upside down."[18] A year later, having won the election, Sirleaf looked beyond her presidency to the legacies she would like to leave Liberia. "We have to take responsibility for our own development. We have to determine that our resources first and foremost will be used for our development. And if we can send that kind of message to our younger generation who will be assuming leadership, you know, over the next few years, then I think the sustainability of our effort will be secured."[19] Translating that vision into a Liberia where citizens truly feel they have the means and authority to shape their own paths remains the challenge.

Sirleaf did much to try to move Liberia forward. The challenge was whether this vision matched the realities of rural Liberia, where people lived within the legal framework of chiefs and societies, somewhat removed from the national legal system and far from any help the state could provide. Could Sirleaf's conventional vision of government, rooted in Western assumptions and structures, offer Liberians the kinds of engagement with governance that would make them feel connected to their government? Only time will tell.

Notes

Introduction

1. "The Nobel Peace Prize for 2011," accessed November 12, 2014, http://www.nobelprize.org/nobel_prizes/peace/laureates/2011/press.html.

2. SCR 1325 focuses on the effects of war on women and urges the inclusion of women in peace negotiations and postconflict reconstruction.

Chapter 1: Growing Up in Two Worlds

1. "History of Liberia: A Time Line," http://memory.loc.gov/ammem/gmdhtml/libhtml/liberia.html.

2. Merran Fraenkel, *Tribe and Class in Monrovia* (published for the International African Institute by Oxford University Press, 1964), 5, 156.

3. "Indirect Rule in the Hinterland," accessed April 17, 2014, www.globalsecurity.org/military/library/report/1985/liberia_1_indirectrulep.htm.

4. Fraenkel, *Tribe and Class in Monrovia,* 119, 25.

5. Ibid., 33, 34, 36, 39.

6. Ibid., 156, 154.

7. Ibid., 152–59.

8. Ellen Johnson Sirleaf, *This Child Will Be Great: Memoir of a Remarkable Life by Africa's First Woman President* (New York: Harper Perennial, 2010), 22.

9. "Monrovia, Liberia: Heritage Landmark of the United Methodist Church," College of West Africa, http://www.gcah.org/research/travelers-guide/college-of-west-africa.

10. Angie E. Brooks, "Political Participation of Women in Africa South of the Sahara," *Annals of the American Academy of Political and Social Science* 375, no. 1 (January 1968): 82–85.

11. Sirleaf, *This Child Will Be Great*, 29–30.

Chapter 2: Scholar and Government Employee

1. Ellen Johnson Sirleaf, *This Child Will Be Great: Memoir of a Remarkable Life by Africa's First Woman President* (New York: Harper Perennial, 2010), 7.

2. Cecil Franweah Frank, "A Critical Look at the Role of the Diaspora in Liberia's Development," *Liberian Dialogue,* last updated January 3, 2013, http://theliberiandialogue.org/2013/01/03/a-critical-look-at-the-role-of-the-diaspora-in-liberias-development.

3. "Liberia: America's Impoverished Orphan in Africa," *Washington Post,* accessed April 17, 2014, http://media.washingtonpost.com/wp-adv/specialsales/international/spotlight/liberia/article2.html.

4. Merran Fraenkel, *Tribe and Class in Monrovia* (published for the International African Institute by Oxford University Press, 1964), 61.

5. Lawrence A. Marinelli, "Liberia's Open-Door Policy," *Journal of Modern African Studies* 2, no. 1 (1964): 91–98.

6. Cited in Harold D. Nelson, *Liberia: Country Study* (Federal Research Division of the Library of Congress, 1985), http://www.globalsecurity.org/military/library/report/1985/liberia_1_opendoor.htm.

7. Frank, "Critical Look at the Role of the Diaspora."

8. Sirleaf, *This Child Will Be Great*, 81.

9. Fred P. M. van der Kraaij, "Iron Ore: The Start of Operations of Liberia's First Iron Ore Mine," *Liberia: Past and Present of Africa's Oldest Republic,* last updated May 2015, http://www.liberiapastandpresent.org/ODP/IronOre/IronOreC.htm.

10. Sirleaf, *This Child Will Be Great*, 71.

11. Siahyonkron Nyanseor, "Putting the Matilda Newport Myth to Rest, Part I," *Perspective,* December 1, 2003, http://www.theperspective.org/december2003/newportmyth.html.

12. Helene Cooper, *The House at Sugar Beach: In Search of a Lost African Childhood* (New York: Simon and Schuster, 2008), 11.

Chapter 3: Liberian Opportunities and International Perils

1. County Development Committee, *Grand Gedeh County Development Agenda, Republic of Liberia, 2008–2012* (Republic of Liberia, n.d.), 1.

2. "President Samuel K. Doe, 1980–1990: The Master-Sergeant President," http://www.liberiapastandpresent.org/SamuelKDoe.htm.

3. Helene Cooper, *The House at Sugar Beach: In Search of a Lost African Childhood* (New York: Simon and Schuster, 2008), 182.

4. Leymah Gbowee, *Mighty Be Our Powers: How Sisterhood, Prayer, and Sex Changed a Nation at War* (New York: Beast Books, 2011), 9.

5. "Remarks of the President and Head of State Samuel K. Doe of Liberia Following Their Meetings: August 17, 1982," University of Texas, http://www.reagan.utexas.edu/archives/speeches/1982/81782d.htm.

6. "Liberia and the United States: A Complex Relationship," *Global Connections: Liberia,* WGBH Educational Foundation, last updated 2002, http://www.pbs.org/wgbh/globalconnections/liberia/essays/uspolicy.

7. Ellen Johnson Sirleaf, *This Child Will Be Great: Memoir of a Remarkable Life by Africa's First Woman President* (New York: Harper Perennial, 2010), 128.

8. Terry Atlas, "Shultz Visit to Liberia a Bit Sour," *Chicago Tribune,* January 15, 1987,

9. David K. Shipler, "Shultz Is under Fire for Asserting Liberia Has Made Gains on Rights," *New York Times,* last updated January 16, 1987, http://www.nytimes.com/1987/01/16/world/shultz-is-under-fire-for-asserting-libria-has-made-gains-on-rights.html.

10. "Charles Taylor 'Worked' for CIA in Liberia," BBC News, January 19, 2012, http://www.bbc.co.uk/news/world-africa-16627628.

11. "My Verbal Sparring with Charles Taylor," BBC News, last updated April 26, 2012, http://www.bbc.com/news/world-africa-17845592.

12. Shelly Dick, "FMO Country Guide: Liberia," accessed June 1, 2015, http://www.forcedmigration.org/research-resources/expert-guides/liberia/fmo013.pdf.

13. US House of Representatives, "US Policy and the Crisis in Liberia," Hearing before the Subcommittee on Africa of the Committee on Foreign Affairs. 101st Congress, 2nd Session, June 19, 1990, http://babel.hathitrust.org/cgi/pt?id=pst.000017170666;view=1up;seq=1.

14. Michael R. Gordon, "US Forces Evacuate 74 after Threats in Liberia," *New York Times,* August 6, 1990, http://www.nytimes.com/1990/08/06/world/us-forces-evacuate-74-after-threats-in-liberia.html.

15. The Carter Center, "Observing the 1997 Special Elections," https://www.cartercenter.org/documents/electionreports/democracy/FinalReportLiberia1997.pdf; Howard French, citing Amos Sawyer in "US Wins Liberians' Pledge to Back Truce," http://www.nytimes.com/1996/04/26/world/us-wins-liberians-pledge-to-back-truce.html.

16. "Rwanda: OAU Report, 07/07/00," last updated July 7, 2000, http://www.africa.upenn.edu/Urgent_Action/apic-070800.html

17. Carter Center, "Observing the 1997 Elections," 45.

18. Sirleaf, *This Child Will Be Great*, 221.

19. Anna Schecter, "Prosecutor: Pat Robertson Had Gold Deal with African Dictator," ABC News, February 4, 2010, http://abcnews.go.com/Blotter/pat-robertsons-gold-deal-african-dictator/story?id=9749341.

20. Sirleaf, *This Child Will Be Great*, 219, 221.

21. International Crisis Group, *Liberia: The Key to Ending Regional Instability*, April 24, 2002, http://www.crisisgroup.org/~/media/Files/africa/west-africa/liberia/Liberia%20The%20Key%20to%20Ending%20Regional%20Instability.pdf.

22. "Ellen Johnson-Sirleaf Returns Home, Meets with Taylor Today," *Perspective*, September 24, 2001.

23. "'Taylor Responds to Pressure,' Says Ellen Johnson-Sirleaf," *Perspective*, August 4, 2001.

24. International Crisis Group, *Liberia: The Key to Ending Regional Instability*, 16.

25. Ibid., 19.

26. Marlise Simons, "Ex-President of Liberia Aided War Crimes, Court Rules," *New York Times*, last updated April 26, 2012, http://www.nytimes.com/2012/04/27/world/africa/charles-taylor-liberia-sierra-leone-war-crimes-court-verdict.html?pagewanted=all.

27. Abdoulaye W. Dukulé, "Liberia: Sirleaf to Chair Commission on Good Governance: 'We Can't Slip Back,'" *AllAfrica*, last updated November 12, 2003, http://allafrica.com/stories/200311120271.html.

Chapter 4: Women and Postconflict Liberia

1. Elizabeth Rehn and Ellen Johnson Sirleaf, "Women, War, and Peace: The Independent Experts' Assessment on the Impact of Armed Conflict on Women and Women's Role in Peace," UNIFEM (2002), vii, http://www.unwomen.org/en/digital-library/publications/2002/1/women-war-peace-the-independent-experts-assessment-on-the-impact-of-armed-conflict-on-women-and-women-s-role-in-peace-building-progress-of-the-world-s-women-2002-vol-1.

2. Leymah Gbowee, *Mighty Be Our Powers: How Sisterhood, Prayer, and Sex Changed a Nation at War* (New York: Beast Books, 2011), 167.

3. Marquette University, "Honorary Degree Recipient: Her Excellency Ellen Johnson Sirleaf," October 23, 2006, http://www.marquette.edu/universityhonors/honors_sirleaf.shtml.

4. Ellen Johnson Sirleaf, *This Child Will Be Great: Memoir of a Remarkable Life by Africa's First Woman President* (New York: Harper Perennial, 2010), 244.

5. Gbowee, *Mighty Be Our Powers*, 169.

6. Sirleaf, *This Child Will Be Great*, 251.

7. Ibid., 252.

8. Andrew Rice, "George Weah's New Game," *New York Times,* August 21, 2005, http://www.nytimes.com/2005/08/21/magazine /21WEAH.html?pagewanted=all&_r=0.

9. United Nations, "Liberia: Elections Mark Historic Turning Point," *Major Peacekeeping Operations,* accessed August 2, 2014, http:// www.un.org/en/peacekeeping/publications/yir/2005/PDFs/major _pk_operations.pdf.

10. Lydia Polgreen, "In First for Africa, Woman Wins Election as President of Liberia," *New York Times,* last updated November 12, 2005, http://www.nytimes.com/2005/11/12/international/africa/12liberia .html?pagewanted=all.

11. US House of Representatives, "Text of Congratulating President Ellen Johnson-Sirleaf for Becoming the First Democratically Elected Female President of the Republic of Liberia and the First Female African Head of State," H.Con Res. 327 (109th Congress, 2005–2006), December 18, 2005, https://www.govtrack.us/congress /bills/109/hconres327/text.

12. Philip Marcelo, "Rebuilding Liberia: Chafee Recalls Liberia's First Post War Election," last updated August 2, 2013, http:// www.providencejournal.com/breaking-news/content/20130802 -rebuilding-liberia-chafee-recalls-liberia-s-first-post-war-election.ece.

Chapter 5: President Sirleaf

1. "Liberia: Text of Inaugural Address by President Ellen Johnson Sirleaf of Liberia," *All Africa*, January 17, 2006, http://allafrica.com /stories/200601170106.html.

2. "Liberia's Ellen Johnson-Sirleaf Addresses Congress," *PBS Newshour,* last updated March 15, 2006, http://www.pbs.org/newshour /bb/africa-jan-june06-liberia_3-15/.

3. Ellen Johnson Sirleaf, *This Child Will Be Great: Memoir of a Remarkable Life by Africa's First Woman President* (New York: Harper Perennial, 2010), 295.

4. Dorsey & Whitney LLP, "Liberia Is Not Ready: A Report of Country Conditions in Liberia and Reasons the United States Should Not End Temporary Protected Status for Liberians," for Minnesota

Advocates for Human Rights (August 2007), dorsey.com/files/upload /DorseyProBonoReport0807Liberia_is_not_Ready.pdf.

5. UNMIL, "Liberia: UNMIL Humanitarian Situation Report No. 110," July 1, 2007, http://reliefweb.int/report/liberia/liberia-unmil -humanitarian-situation-report-no-110.

6. Government Printing Office, "Country Reports on Human Rights Practices," 2008, 335.

7. *The New Dawn,* transcript of interview with President Ellen Johnson Sirleaf, Paynesville, Monday, July 1, 2013, http://www .thenewdawnliberia.com/~thenewd1/index.php?option=com_content &view=article&id=1798:weah-warns-supporters&catid=25:politics &Itemid=59.

8. Peace A. Medie, "Fighting Gender-Based Violence: The Women's Movement and the Enforcement of Rape Law in Liberia," *African Affairs* 112, no. 448 (2013): 377–97.

9. Stéphanie Vig, "The Liberian Rape Amendment Act and the United Nations: A Critical Evaluation of the Law-Making Process" (MPhil thesis, Balliol College, Oxford University, 2007).

10. The Liberian TRC final report is accessible at http:// trcofliberia.org/reports/final-report.

11. Marie-Claire O. Omanyondo, "Sexual Gender-Based Violence and Health Faculity Needs Assessment (Montserrado and Bong Counties), Liberia," World Health Organization, September 6–21, 2004, 18, http://www.who.int/hac/crises/lbr/Liberia_GBV_2004 _FINAL.pdf?ua=1.

12. "Witness Jesus Swaray: 'I Saw Madam Sirleaf in Military Uniform,'" Truth and Reconciliation Commission of Liberia Website, http://trcofliberia.org/press_releases/115.

13. Sirleaf, *This Child Will Be Great,* 174–76.

14. "Ellen: I Have Absolutely Not Supported Any Warring Faction," January 12, 2009, Truth and Reconciliation Commission of Liberia Website, http://trcofliberia.org/press_releases/28.

15. "A Conversation with Ellen Johnson Sirleaf," Council on Foreign Relations, November 28, 2012, http://www.cfr.org/liberia /conversation-Sirleaf-johnson-sirleaf/p29177.

16. Prue Clarke and Emily Schmall, "Liberia's Election: Hard Times for Ellen Johnson Sirleaf," http://www.newsweek.com /liberias-election-hard-times-ellen-johnson-sirleaf-68251

17. "Sirleaf Does Not Deserve Nobel Prize, Say Weah, Tubman," Reuters, October 7, 2011, http://www.reuters.com/article/2011/10/07 /us-nobel-liberia-idUSTRE7966HW20111007.

Conclusion

1. "Liberia: Probing the 'Bad Deeds' of the Sirleaf-led Govt," *All Africa,* April 22, 2013, accessed May 17, 2015, http://allafrica.com/stories/201304222102.html.

2. Seltue R. Karweaye, "All in the Family: African President's Children Succession, Is Liberia Next?," *Front Page Africa,* July 18, 2014, http://frontpageafricaonline.com/index.php/op-ed/commentaries-features/2343-all-in-the-family-african-president-s-children-succeession-is-liberia-next.

3. "George Weah Wins Seat in Liberia's Senate," *Guardian,* December 28, 2014, http://www.theguardian.com/world/2014/dec/28/george-weah-wins-seat-liberia-senate-monrovia.

4. James Giahyue, "Liberia Justice Minister Quits, Says President Blocked Investigation," October 7, 2014, http://www.reuters.com/article/2014/10/07/us-liberia-politics-idUSKCN0HW17220141007.

5. Council on Foreign Relations, "A Conversation with Ellen Johnson Sirleaf," May 25, 2010, http://www.cfr.org/liberia/conversation-ellen-johnson-sirleaf/p34766.

6. "Rape: Liberia's New War" *Malay Mail Online,* June 8, 2014, http://www.themalaymailonline.com/features/article/rape-liberias-new-war#sthash.iAMAqSJg.dpuf.

7. Amnesty International, *Amnesty International Report 2011: The State of the World's Human Rights* (London: Amnesty International, 2011), 209.

8. Blair Glencorse, "Liberia Ten Years On—Corruption and Accountability Remain Country's Biggest Challenges," August 16, 2013, http://owcl.wordpress.com/2013/08/16/liberia-ten-years-on-corruption-and-accountability-remain-countrys-biggest-challenges/.

9. Global Witness, "Signing Their Lives Away: Liberia's Private Use Permits and the Destruction of Community-Owned Rainforest," September 2012.

10. Bernard Gbayee Goah, "War Crimes Court for Liberia Is Necessary," December 2, 2013, https://owcl.wordpress.com/2013/12/02/war-crimes-court-for-liberia-is-necessary/.

11. "Transcript of Interview with H. E. President Ellen Johnson Sirleaf," July 1, 2013, http://www.emansion.gov.lr/doc/Transcript_of_Interview%20with_HE_President_ELBC.pdf.

12. "Liberia Declares State of Emergency over Ebola Virus," BBC News, August 7, 2014, http://www.bbc.com/news/world-28684561.

13. Cerue Konah Garlo, "Liberia Cannot Cope with Ebola," August 20, 2014, http://www.cnn.com/2014/08/20/opinion/garlo-ebola-liberia/index.html.

14. Al-Varney Rogers, "Liberia: CDC Boss Bemoans Liberia—'Worst Ever Ebola Outbreak,'" August 28, 2014, accessed May 15, 2015, http://allafrica.com/stories/201408281197.html.

15. Centers for Disease Control and Prevention, "Morbidity and Mortality Weekly Report (MMWR)," November 21, 2014, http://www.cdc.gov/mmwr/preview/mmwrhtml/mm6346a8.htm.

16. "Ebola in Perspective: The Role of Popular Music in Crisis Situations in West Africa," *Africa Is a Country,* http://africasacountry.com/2014/10/ebola-in-perspective/; "How to Make a Hit Song about Ebola," *Atlantic,* August 25, 2014.

17. Rick Gladstone, "Liberian Leader Concedes Errors in Response to Ebola," March 11, 2015, accessed May 15, 2015, http://www.nytimes.com/2015/03/12/world/africa/liberian-leader-concedes-errors-in-response-to-ebola.html?_r=0.

18. Prue Clarke and Emily Schmall, "Liberia's Election: Hard Times for Ellen Johnson Sirleaf," October 2, 2011, http://www.newsweek.com/liberias-election-hard-times-ellen-johnson-sirleaf-68251.

19. Council on Foreign Relations, "A Conversation with Ellen Johnson Sirleaf," September 28, 2012, http://www.cfr.org/liberia/conversation-Sirleaf-johnson-sirleaf/p29177.

Selected Bibliography

Brooks, Angie E. "Political Participation of Women in Africa South of the Sahara." *Annals of the American Academy of Political and Social Science* 375, no. 1 (January 1968): 82–85.

The Carter Center. "Observing the 1997 Special Elections Process in Liberia." https://www.cartercenter.org/documents/electionreports/democracy/FinalReportLiberia1997.pdf.

Cooper, Helene. *The House at Sugar Beach: In Search of a Lost African Childhood.* New York: Simon and Schuster, 2008.

County Development Committee. *Grand Gedeh County Development Agenda, Republic of Liberia, 2008–2012.* Republic of Liberia, n.d. http://www.mia.gov.lr/doc/Grand%20Gedeh%20CDA_web.pdf.

Dukulé, Abdoulaye W. "Liberia: Sirleaf to Chair Commission on Good Governance: 'We Can't Slip Back.'" *AllAfrica*, November 12, 2003. http://allafrica.com/stories/200311120271.htm.

Fraenkel, Merran. *Tribe and Class in Monrovia.* Published for the International African Institute by Oxford University Press, 1964.

Frank, Cecil Franweah. "A Critical Look at the Role of the Diaspora in Liberia's Development." *Liberian Dialogue,* last updated January 3, 2013, http://theliberiandialogue.org/2013/01/03/a-critical-look-at-the-role-of-the-diaspora-in-liberias-development.

Fuest, Veronika. "Liberia's Women Acting for Peace: Collective Action in a War-Affected Country." In *Movers and Shakers: Social Movements in Africa,* edited by Stephen Ellis and Ineke Van Kessel, 114–37. Boston: Brill, 2009.

Gbowee, Leymah, with Carol Mithers. *Mighty Be Our Powers: How Sisterhood, Prayer, and Sex Changed a Nation at War.* New York: Beast Books, 2011.

International Crisis Group. *Liberia: The Key to Ending Regional Instability.* Africa Report No. 43. Freetown/Brussels, 2002. http://www.crisisgroup.org/~/media/Files/africa/west-africa/liberia

/Liberia%20The%20Key%20to%20Ending%20Regional%20
Instability.pdf.

Liberia Truth and Reconciliation Commission. Final Report. http://
trcofliberia.org/reports/final-report.

Marcelo, Philip. "Rebuilding Liberia: Chafee Recalls Liberia's First
Post War Election." *Providence Journal,* August 2, 2013. http://
www.providencejournal.com/breaking-news/content/20130802
-rebuilding-liberia-chafee-recalls-liberia-s-first-post-war
-election.ece.

Marinelli, Lawrence A. "Liberia's Open-Door Policy." *Journal of Modern African Studies* 2, no. 1 (1964): 91–98.

Marquette University. "Honorary Degree Recipient: Her Excellency
Ellen Johnson Sirleaf." October 23, 2006. http://www.marquette
.edu/universityhonors/honors_sirleaf.shtml.

Medie, Peace A. "Fighting Gender-Based Violence: The Women's Movement and the Enforcement of Rape Law in Liberia." *African Affairs* 112, no. 448 (2013): 377–97.

Moran, Mary H. *Civilized Women: Gender and Prestige in Southeastern
Liberia.* Ithaca, NY: Cornell University Press, 1990.

———. *Liberia: The Violence of Democracy.* Philadelphia: University
of Pennsylvania Press, 2006.

Nyanseor, Siahyonkron. "Putting the Matilda Newport Myth to Rest,
Part I." *Perspective,* December 1, 2003. http://www.theperspective
.org/december2003/newportmyth.html.

Rehn, Elizabeth, and Ellen Johnson Sirleaf. "Women, War, and Peace: The
Independent Experts' Assessment on the Impact of Armed Conflict
on Women and Women's Role in Peace." UNIFEM (2002). http://
www.unwomen.org/en/digital-library/publications/2002/1
/women-war-peace-the-independent-experts-assessment-on
-the-impact-of-armed-conflict-on-women-and-women-s-role
-in-peace-building-progress-of-the-world-s-women-2002-vol-1.

Sirleaf, Ellen Johnson. *This Child Will Be Great: Memoir of a Remarkable Life by Africa's First Woman President.* New York: Harper
Perennial, 2010.

Tripp, Aili. "Regional Networking as Transnational Feminism." African Gender Institute. http://agi.ac.za/sites/agi.ac.za/files/fa_4
_feature_article_3.pdf.

United Nations. "Liberia: Elections Mark Historic Turning Point."
Major Peacekeeping Operations, 2005. http://www.un.org/en
/peacekeeping/publications/yir/2005/PDFs/major_pk
_operations.pdf.

United States House of Representatives. "US Policy and the Crisis in Liberia." Hearing before the Subcommittee on Africa of the Committee on Foreign Affairs. 101st Congress, 2nd Session, June 19, 1990. http://babel.hathitrust.org/cgi/pt?id=pst.000017170666 ;view=1up;seq=1.

van der Kraaij, Fred P. M. "Iron Ore: The Start of Operations of Liberia's First Iron Ore Mine." *Liberia: Past and Present of Africa's Oldest Republic.* http://www.liberiapastandpresent.org/ODP/IronOre /IronOreC.htm.

———. "President Charles D. B. King (1920–1930): The 1926 Firestone Concession Agreement." *Liberia: Past and Present of Africa's Oldest Republic.* http://www.liberiapastandpresent.org /1926FirestoneCA.htm.

Vig, Stéphanie. "The Liberian Rape Amendment Act and the United Nations: A Critical Evaluation of the Law-Making Process." MPhil thesis, Balliol College, Oxford University, 2007.

Index

126

CPSIA information can be obtained
at www.ICGtesting.com
Printed in the USA
LVHW080206160819
627869LV00013B/222/P